NURTURING THE LIGHT INSIDE

SHERRY DANNER

NURTURING THE LIGHT INSIDE

OVERCOMING ADDICTION AND CODEPENDENCY ON THE PATH TO SELF-LOVE

Autumn Walk Books

Published by Autumn Walk Books, Douglass, Kansas
www.nurturedlight.com

Edited and designed by Girl Friday Productions
www.girlfridayproductions.com

Design: Paul Barrett
Project management: Sara Spees Addicott
Image credits: cover © Shutterstock/suns07butterfly

ISBN (paperback): 978-1-7350622-0-4
ISBN (ebook): 978-1-7350622-1-1
Library of Congress Control Number: 2020910142

First edition

For those starting on the path to self-love . . .
may the light of others guide your way.

"When we realize we've had duct tape over our mouths for decades, there is only one thing to do: tear it off. Our power is not in blaming or shaming, but in waking up from the collective trance in which we've been living."

—Geneen Roth, *This Messy Magnificent Life*

CONTENTS

Part II: Further Insights and Practical Application

A NOTE FROM
THE AUTHOR

As a heartbroken and healing person, I find other heartbroken and healing people easiest to love. Sometimes even these people run a close second to animals, the easiest to love of all. Many of you will understand. Even when we enter this world fiercely loved, as I did, life can break our tender hearts early and often. A vast majority of us are recovering from something by the time we're well into adulthood. And experiencing a measure of shame—feeling less than or not good enough—is part of the human experience.

Some of us further contribute to this stockpiling of emotional traumas in our lives through compulsive behaviors and questionable relationship choices. And those of us who do so face an especially crippling brand of shame. If we're courageous enough to face that shame and fight for our own lives, we can find ourselves not only recovering but also experiencing the state of being *in recovery*—that ongoing process of deep reflection, rigorous accountability, and intentional emotional growth. The heartbroken and healing people who are in recovery are my favorites.

I admit that I'm biased because I'm in recovery myself: from addictions to food and alcohol, and from codependency. I've spent many years unlearning damaging beliefs and habits, processing the lingering effects of trauma and self-neglect, and releasing toxic shame. Over time, I've learned to care about myself, to allow others to help me, to practice the art of authenticity, and to set and hold healthy boundaries—all of which are the simple, but not easy, cures to self-destruction.

Born with white skin into a loving, middle-class family and a body free of disease or disability, I've lived a privileged life. Yet despite my stable upbringing, and to my own consternation, self-destructive behavior came to me with remarkable ease. Freeing myself from my inner battles and the consequences of my choices was the tough part.

I share the stories in this book not because my situations were unique but because the phenomenon of experiencing cascading failures in a life that started with great promise is, sadly, so common.

Perfectionistic thinking and harsh self-judgment today have a great impact on young people in our culture. I'm interested in shining a light on this by sharing what that life-sucking way of thinking did to me. While working to conquer my decades-long addictions to food and alcohol, I discovered that my core underlying problem was a lack of self-love. This struggle to love myself, even though I was loved, led to an unhealthy relationship pattern that I refer to as codependency.

Codependency is, I know, a confusing and frequently misunderstood term. It took me years of personal and professional study to understand codependency in a way that's helpful for recovery. For those who are interested, I've included a more in-depth discussion of my take on the term in chapter 11. There are countless books and theories out there about the origins of addiction and codependency. That is not the subject of this book. This is not an exploration of why addiction and codependency occur, but rather a collection of stories about what addiction and codependency looked like for me and how I overcame them.

Regarding the question of why these things happen to some people and not others, I'll simply say that for complex and varied reasons, many of us don't learn how to deal with our anxiety and other confusing emotions in a healthy way. As teenagers and young adults, some of us turn to substances and behaviors that provide immediate soothing—food, alcohol, drugs, video games, and, at increasing rates, internet pornography. If our reliance on substances or numbing activities to manage our inner worlds becomes habitual over time, these coping strategies can fail us spectacularly by becoming full-blown addictions.

Addiction leaves us with only two options: to self-destruct or accept help and learn a new way to cope with our thoughts and emotions. Those of us who (eventually) choose the second option go through the excruciating, humbling process of facing our heartbrokenness. Through a recovery process, we learn how to feel our feelings, manage our thoughts, and connect meaningfully with others through mutual vulnerability. We learn to accept our own humanness rather than harshly judge ourselves—that judgment having created the need to escape in the first place. Once we do this, we can start rebuilding our lives. Though I'm not proud of all my past behaviors, I am proud to be one of those rebuilders. And after more than a decade of rebuilding, I'm most proud of the fact that I find it easy to love myself now, too.

Shame fuels self-destructive behavior, and secrets are the breeding ground for shame. In a culture in which abuses by powerful individuals and institutions are exposed regularly, I've grown leery of those who encourage silence. For that reason, I'm more in favor of public sharing than I used to be. Sometimes the only power we have is our words and stories.

To that end, the personal reflection questions after each chapter in part 1 are provided to encourage you to consider, discuss, and even write down your own stories. I admire writers like Glennon Doyle and Roxane Gay, who model courage by writing about their most painful moments. Following their example allows us to expose difficult truths about our society and help each other to feel less alone.

I've shared a few of my rawest moments in these pages in support of that effort. I invite you now to join me in locking hands with these brave souls as we walk in solidarity toward the silencers—all of us, together, an unstoppable army of peaceful warriors.

INTRODUCTION

Our stories matter—especially the messy ones. The stories we wish had never happened, the ones we hide or stuff down so far that we *almost* forget them, may be the ones that matter most of all. They matter most because within them we've tucked away our deepest shame.

That shame, the feeling of being unworthy and unlovable, keeps us from letting others in. But we must learn to let others in, because shame is powerful only when allowed to fester alone in the dark. We aren't even aware that it's there, but shame shapes our beliefs about ourselves and shows itself in our life choices. Unattended shame causes us to abandon ourselves and go in search of validation from outside sources that never meet our deepest needs. When we engage in self-destructive behavior, attach ourselves to people who don't have the capacity to love us back, or neglect ourselves to the point that we don't really know who we are at all, shame is the cause, and feelings of loneliness and despair are the result.

In the pages that follow, I share stories of how I learned to love myself and to set healthy boundaries. This change means that my thoughts and actions now reflect a belief in my own inherent worth. I no longer sacrifice my well-being to please others.

The first section, part 1, is an account of my personal experiences and meant to offer hope. The chapters are stand-alone essays, snapshots of memories. They provide glimpses rather than a complete, chronological story. Some names and details have been changed to protect others' privacy. Those who were involved in these events will naturally have differing perspectives about them. That's how personal experience and memory work. I'm not writing to comment on anyone's life and journey but my own.

A brief note about the treatment of spirituality in these pages: My experience and my writing reflect a spiritual journey more than they do a religious one. By this I mean that you won't find biblical references here, though I do describe my personal relationship with a benign presence known to me as God. I'm a Christian, though I admit to sometimes feeling apologetic about the label these days. Sadly, it has come to represent a way of thinking about important cultural issues that does not align with my core beliefs. My faith is unwavering, but my relationship with organized religion is far more complicated. I'm still working that out. I'm grateful to have found a church that welcomes my questions, and I love the people and the pastors there, even as I detest the patriarchy. As a heterosexual Christian, I want to be clear that I'm a staunch supporter of the LGBTQ+ community. The Christ I aim to follow teaches inclusion and acceptance of all human souls equally.

On the topic of alcohol-addiction recovery, within these pages I discuss an alternative non-twelve-step path that led me to freedom from dependence on alcohol. Discussion of this nontraditional approach may elicit a strong response from some readers who have their own thoughts about the efficacy of various treatment approaches. It's not my intention to either condemn or recommend any recovery process or organization. My goal is to spotlight the fact that not everyone recovers the same way.

Like most who awaken from the nightmare of addiction and/or codependency, I can clearly see now that for many years I lived with a lot of hidden shame and a disconnection from myself so familiar and constant I didn't even recognize it was there. I have experienced for myself and seen hundreds of clients experience the shame-reducing power of allowing another human being to peer inside our inner worlds—inner worlds that we're convinced contain proof that we're unworthy. Loving acceptance, offered from one human being to another, shines the light that drives away shame. This is how we save each other.

The far more difficult task is learning how to nurture that light within ourselves—to love ourselves the way God loves us, which is not just when we're "being good" but *always*. Only once we learn to do this can we experience the joy of being alive.

This is not the same thing as being happy all the time. We're not meant to be happy all the time. We're meant to be *experiencing* all the time. A good portion of that experience, for all of us, without exception, will be painful. Until we cultivate a self-love that can carry us through those painful parts, our lives will be much harder than they were intended to be.

If you need a starting place on the path to self-love, begin with offering yourself some patience for the fact that you aren't there yet. Patience and love are close buddies. Invite one in and the other one's likely to show up, too.

PART I

Stories and Personal
Reflection Questions

How to Use the Personal Reflection Questions

From early childhood, we begin taking in information about ourselves from the world. With our still developing minds, we form ideas about our worth and our capacities. So often, these ideas are not based on truth, but we believe them for so long that we mistake them for *facts*. Even after we realize logically that they aren't facts, replacing these false beliefs with new truths requires some work. No other work you do in your lifetime may be as important. Discovering what you truly believe about yourself at the deepest, subconscious level and then purposely *choosing* beliefs instead of accepting ones that are simply there by default will reshape your life.

The personal reflection questions at the end of each chapter offer you a way to learn more about yourself—and, if you use them in a safe group, more about each other—and are intended to encourage you to nurture the light inside of you. You may prefer to ponder them privately or journal about them, or you may choose to share your responses with a friend or review them with a therapist or coach.

Important Note: Reading about shame and trauma and/or considering your own shame and trauma can trigger PTSD symptoms such as anxiety, insomnia, self-harm impulses, and feelings of social isolation. I highly recommend working with a trained mental health professional when examining your personal history and beliefs about yourself, especially if this is new territory for you. The personal reflection questions won't be appropriate for or useful to everyone for a variety of reasons. Please take care of yourself. Reach out to loved ones or a professional for support if the questions create distress for you. Each person's path is unique, but we all deserve support and encouragement along the way.

CHAPTER ONE

Mute and Screaming

I am in my childhood home in Wichita, Kansas, visiting my parents, when the news story breaks. An anonymous woman has come forward with an accusation of sexual assault against a Supreme Court justice nominee. The details are sketchy, but both the woman and man were in high school when the alleged incident occurred.

The six o'clock news blares from the television. The volume on the remote is broken, and now has only two settings: mute or screaming. To my mom's consternation, my sharp-minded eighty-six-year-old father, an extremely handy former engineer who can still fix anything he wants to fix, seems content to live with the effects of the malfunction.

In the fall of 2018, stories of sexual assault allegations appear frequently on the news. I intentionally pay little attention to the announcement, despite my immediate interest. I decide I'll read the story later that night at home on my iPad. As a rule, I don't

discuss the sordid realities of life—mine or others'—
with my parents.

Dad is completely silent, which is how he watches
the news. It is how he does most things. I understand because I am like him in this way. My mom
frequently manages the silence by talking to herself.

"For goodness sake! Over something that happened in high school? Really?" she says now to no
one.

I don't respond. Avoiding political discussions
works best for us, allowing our family to get along
extremely well. My parents are the definition of con-
servative. Born in Oklahoma in the 1930s, they were
raised to live simply and to keep personal matters
private. They're kind, responsible, hardworking, salt-
of-the-earth folks who devoted their lives to raising
my two older sisters and me. By some combination
of love, parental wisdom, and a shared natural aversion to conflict, we coexist peacefully, even though
I, their youngest daughter, am a feminist and pas-
sionate social justice advocate. Most of the time, we
dance around these differences with relative ease.

But my mother's unfiltered thought has escaped
into the living room, and I have difficulty letting it
float past as I normally would. This tiny shift inside
unsettles me. If our unspoken contract of mutual
tolerance can be disrupted by my reactivity to

comments like this, our tidy little system may be in jeopardy.

It takes me a second to understand why this time her words have penetrated my protective inner shield. A current student in an MFA in creative writing program, I have earlier this very day finished writing a piece about my own sexual assault in high school. My parents have no idea this assault happened to me, and of course they have no idea that I am writing about it.

I glance over at my sweet-natured, blessedly healthy eighty-one-year-old mother. Will she say the same thing if she ever reads my story? *For goodness sake! Over something that happened in high school? Really?*

At the time of this visit with my parents, I'm on the cusp of turning fifty, and I've never been happier in my entire life. I recently chucked my big-city life and purchased a restored Victorian home in a tiny rural town forty-five minutes from the house where I grew up and where my parents still live. I wanted to live closer to them in their precious final years, but I wasn't crazy about heading directly back into the heart of my own history. Close but not too close, this quaint bedroom community offered a sweet compromise, and I took a glorious midlife leap.

Once I'm home the next day, I take time to catch up on the news. The accusation of sexual assault against Supreme Court justice nominee Brett Kavanaugh has blown up overnight and captured the nation's rapt attention. I cuddle up on my sofa in front of the TV with my fluffy little dog, Maslow, in my new/old house in my new little town where I am happy.

Watching Christine Blasey Ford tell her story, I feel psychically connected to the countless other victims of sexual assault who must be watching. I imagine them experiencing with me a delighted disbelief at the rare exposure of dirty secrets bred by a culture of toxic masculinity. And I ache for those who may feel retraumatized by the airing of details that echo their own history of abuse. I hope the other survivors are soaking in the public validation I, and perhaps they, so needed: Christine Blasey Ford's public declaration that attending a party and drinking beer is not punishable by being sexually used and discarded like a dirty tissue. Do other viewers also feel a vague sense of hope for possible cultural change, even as we collectively relive our individual buried traumas? I am riveted by the details of Dr. Blasey Ford's story, noting the similarities to my own.

. . .

It was in the early '80s, around the time I turned fifteen, that boys started looking at me differently. Cute boys, popular boys, football player boys. Before, I'd gone unnoticed. Now, their eyes lingered on my body, and when I caught them, they held eye contact a few seconds too long, smiling awkwardly.

For a formerly chubby, bushy-haired, bookish girl, this shift was both exciting and disconcerting. I started working out, donning the requisite Jane Fonda aerobics attire—satiny tights and brightly colored dance leotards—and leg-lifted my way to firmness with the rest of the country. And with substantial effort, my unruly hair morphed into something that passed for stylish, thanks to Madonna.

At a party late in the summer of 1984, I witnessed a group of male classmates watching Madonna dance seductively in her "Like a Virgin" video, and this awakened in me a growing understanding of the raw power of female sexuality. They were mesmerized as they watched, practically panting, too immature to attempt to hide their desire.

I had never seen anything like the trance these boys fell into when watching her, had never wanted anything as badly as I wanted those boys to pay attention to me in that same way. Yes, I was beginning to be noticed. But the secret power that commanded something from boys—something that looked to me like respect—still eluded me. The good news was that my big, crazy hair was suddenly an asset instead of an embarrassment, and I was feeling hopeful about starting high school in the fall.

Earlier that summer, in a shocking turn of events, I'd snagged the cutest boy at camp, an older boy named Craig. He was eighteen, a fact that made up for his boyish, obnoxiously crude sense of humor. That sweltering week at Westminster Woods Camp, we snuck away every chance we could to make out behind the cabins or in secret hideaways within the tick-infested woods.

When camp ended, our love affair remained fully alive in my mind, and I enjoyed a summer-long, angsty teenage romance with this older boy who lived far across town and was suddenly remarkably busy, according to his mother, every time I called. I saw him only a couple of times after camp but thought about him constantly. Once it became clear to me that he was not thinking about me nearly as much, I began to channel my yearning instead into writing sappy poetry while listening to *Purple Rain.*

All summer long I slathered my skin with Johnson's baby oil and misted my hair with Sun In or lemon juice to turn my mousy brown into beachy blond. I baked on an old terry cloth towel in the backyard sun, John Waite's "Missing You," melancholy perfection for the romantically tortured, playing on a constant loop on Wichita's pop radio station, KEYN.

Every song seemed to be written just for me, inspiring a rich fantasy world where I was the sultry star of all the MTV videos. In other words, I was happy.

I learned about the late-summer party from a friend. A beginning-of-the-school-year bonfire blowout, to be held in a field near the edge of the city. I prayed that it wouldn't be muggy so my hair would cooperate. By some miracle, on the day of the party the humidity was low and the air unseasonably cool for a Kansas evening in August. Perfect-hair weather always boosted my mood. Arriving at the bonfire near dusk, I felt beautiful and more confident than usual, thanks in part to the mercifully dry air and a couple of preparty beers.

The party was in full swing when I saw Jake Langford looking at me in the soft light of the bonfire. Jake had been known as a nice but goofy boy in middle school, but he'd turned downright cute overnight. I barely recognized him. He'd transformed from a gangly goofball to a stocky football player. He had dark, spiky hair and a huge smile. I had always had a crush on him but hadn't ever talked to him. The smile he gave me now was more assured than awkward, and he didn't look away. Someone handed me a bottle of beer, and as I struggled to get the cap off, I had the brilliant idea of approaching Jake for help as a way of starting a conversation.

Walking over to him, I felt uncharacteristically bold, free of the crippling shyness that had been my social calling card up to this point. I felt like I was both me and not me. *Maybe this is the new me?* I heard myself casually ask if he would help me open my beer. As the words left my mouth, I realized I was a little bit tipsy.

Jake smiled toothily. "Sure, come on over here."

He escorted me away from the fire and the crowd, to an area that was even darker. Now we were alone in the empty field, the sound of music and laughter growing softer along with the light from the fire.

My heart rate quickened at the nearness of his muscular body. Romantic summer make-out sessions with my camp boyfriend were fresh in my mind, and I wondered if Jake might try to kiss me.

He did not. Instead, he started talking in an odd, low voice. I didn't understand what he was saying. Quickly and firmly, he pushed me to my knees as he remained standing, then he forced his hard penis into my mouth and began thrusting. In my shock and confusion, and for reasons that took me years to understand and forgive myself for, my instinct wasn't to fight or scream, only to submit. I'd been socialized to be, in the traditional female manner, compliant, pleasing, and accommodating. There was nothing in my nature or upbringing that would impel me to fight. Meanwhile, Jake had been trained in the cultural male ideals of the time, on and off the football field, to be aggressive, to conquer, to dominate.

Almost immediately, he came in my mouth. I spit the stuff out as if it were poison, frantically wiping my tongue with the back of my hand.

I don't recall now if we walked back to the party together or separately. I do remember that he didn't speak to me again for the rest of the night, or for the rest of high school. Or for the rest of our lives.

What I did immediately after I returned to the bonfire is the part of the story that embarrassed me most for years to come, and that later made me wish I could go back in time and stop myself. In the moments after the assault occurred, while still in a stunned state, I stumbled over to a group of popular girls sitting near the fire and announced, in a manner that made me sound proud—something that I was, in that moment, pretending to be—"I just blew Jake Langford." I remember being unsure if I was using the correct terminology. Being good at English was an important part of me, something I counted on. What, I wondered, was the correct way to say *blow job* in the past tense?

No one corrected my grammar. The girls understood exactly what I was saying. One wisely suggested that I might not want to tell everyone the good news. I gathered from her chilly stare that my awesome Madonna hair was now a frizzy mess. A feeling of panic, like the one I had in a recurring dream in which I showed up to school naked, is the last thing I remember from that night.

The day after the party, I went to the grocery store with my older sister. I hadn't told her about the incident. I sensed she wouldn't think the thing that happened to me was as cool as I was trying to pretend it was, and I couldn't face the blame I imagined would be placed on me for being so gullible and irresponsible. I feared that she'd think less of me. Only a slut, I thought she might say, would do what I'd done.

As we entered the store, we ran smack into two of Jake's football teammates. They smiled at us and said a brisk, "Hi."

Though they gave no sign that Jake had told them, in that moment I felt certain they knew what had happened. I also became aware of an inescapable fact: I'd never know for sure who knew, and I'd always wonder. I felt as if there were a brand on my forehead that announced to the world that I was something to be used, a stupid girl, an easy target for any guy interested in quickly and quietly getting off in the dark without having to be bothered with so much as a conversation.

That morning in the grocery store, I understood that the friendly thing to do was to look them in the eye, smile, and say hello. But I couldn't force myself to do any of those things. I looked down and held my breath as we passed by.

• • •

My childhood friend Andrea Bristow, a married mother of two college-aged kids who now lives in Texas, calls me the day after the Ford-Kavanaugh hearings.

Andrea is the only person I remember telling the truth to about what happened to me that summer at the bonfire party. She and I were teenagers, talking in her car late one night, when I told her what Jake Langford had done to me. I was stunned when she told me that he had done something to her, too. She said that she'd been in the back seat of a friend's car with Jake one night, with some other kids in the front seat, when out of the blue he took her hand and put it on his crotch. She said she'd been grossed out by his actions and pulled her hand away immediately. I felt a little bit better after she shared this with me, realizing it wasn't just me that Jake had targeted. But she'd pushed him away, clearly recognizing and telling him that his behavior was weird and creepy in the moment it happened. Why hadn't I?

On the phone now, Andrea tells me that a female classmate of ours recently posted a message on Facebook about being sexually assaulted in high school. No perpetrator was named in the post, but Andrea discovered through a mutual friend that this Facebook friend was referring to Jake Langford. This woman had privately told our friend that Jake held her down with his knees on her shoulders and ejaculated on her face one night when we were all seniors.

Leaning back in my chair, my heart pounds hard as I hear this news from Andrea.

It wasn't just me. I didn't do something bad. I didn't cause it to happen.

The relief is astounding. Then comes the anger, followed immediately by sadness. How many others? Does every high school in America have a Jake? Or multiple Jakes? I try to imagine how many victims Christine Blasey Ford was representing as she stood before the judging masses, bravely sharing her story and allowing me and other victims of assault to sit on our sofas in the quiet safety of our homes and feel validated, affirmed, heard, hopeful.

Andrea tells me that her husband said, "She's lying," as they watched the hearings. His issue was with her lack of total clarity about some details. "When a thing like that happens," he argued, "a person remembers all the details vividly."

Here's what I know. I don't remember the location of the field where Jake assaulted me when I was fifteen. I could never find that place again, though it's likely within thirty miles of where I'm sitting right now as I write. I don't remember exactly how I got to the party, who I went with, or how I got home. I don't remember what I was wearing or what Jake was wearing. I don't remember the date.

I do remember Jake Langford pressing me to the ground and forcing his penis into my mouth without my consent or any signal from me that I wanted that to happen. All these years later, I still don't have the ability to quantify the impact this had on my life, though I do now understand the power of shame.

But in an argument of fact, the invisible scars are the hardest to prove. I remember the girls I approached at the party, and I remember how, because I was young and confused, I lied and told them I'd "blown" Jake Langford, as if it were an act I'd intentionally performed. When I was fifteen, my only goal was to be accepted. I remember the looks on the girls' faces when I made that claim, and I remember the moment I recognized my miscalculation and sensed the imminent decline of my social status. That moment is seared into my memory. And I remember telling my friend Andrea the truth months later: a teenage girl sharing her secrets with a safe friend late into the night.

Dr. Blasey Ford testified all alone with no one to corroborate her story, no one to validate her memories. That was the most awful part for me to watch.

Thank God I told Andrea.

Jake had a problem, not me.

The shame, I tell myself, *is not mine to carry.*

Andrea tried to tell me this when we were young, and she's telling me again now. I understand this fact logically. I tell women this same thing all the time in my professional role as a therapist. *The shame is not yours to carry.* It's so much easier to see this is true when your own body isn't involved.

Something releases from deep inside me as I realize that I finally believe it's true for me, too.

PERSONAL REFLECTION QUESTIONS

Note: Please read "How to Use the Personal Reflection Questions" at the beginning of this book before you begin. You may find that you're carrying feelings of shame, which can include emptiness, anger, anxiety, or a frequent feeling of not being "good enough" as a result of something that happened to you when you were young and/or vulnerable. Especially if you've never talked to anyone about the event or events before, *please* consider reaching out to a safe person—a partner, trusted family member, friend, pastor, therapist, or coach—and sharing as much of your story as you feel comfortable sharing. That's the best starting place.

The questions included below and throughout this book are meant for those who've already processed, to some degree, their most painful childhood events. Even after we do that work, negative beliefs about ourselves may linger as a result of those events, and there can still be more work to do. Recovering from shame and trauma is a layered process and one that can be lengthy for some. Wherever you are in that journey is OK; just start somewhere.

1. How were emotions expressed, discussed, encouraged, or discouraged in your early life and in your family?

2. What "rules" about emotions do you choose to keep or release now as an adult?

3. We all experience feelings of shame from time to time. How does shame show up in your life? What strategies do you use to help you manage those painful moments?

4. Write down three supportive phrases you can say to yourself the next time you experience feelings of shame.

5. What brought you the most joy when you were a teenager?

6. What did you think about yourself when you were a teenager? Which conclusions that you came to about yourself when you were young do you agree or disagree with now?

7. If you could go back in time, what words of encouragement and support would you offer your teenage self?

CHAPTER TWO

A Taste of Freedom

"AA isn't working for me," I told counselor number four. I was sitting on her mushy sofa, pressing my weight to the left, refusing its attempts to pull me toward its unstable center.

"Or, rather," she replied without missing a beat, "*you* are not working *it*."

The energy I'd worked up to assert myself slipped away. *Oh yes, of course. I'm wrong.* I stopped pushing against the old sofa and let it swallow me.

Her take on the situation, like many of the phrases I'd heard in Alcoholics Anonymous, sounded wise and true and catchy. Still I found myself reaching for something I couldn't yet name. I felt trapped between a desperate desire for sobriety and my inability to connect with the twelve steps. The message I heard, the one I pushed against, was: If you are resisting AA in any way, that is a function of your disease and, therefore, isn't to be trusted.

But I wasn't denying my drinking problem, so the talk of denial frustrated me in a way similar to how other aspects of AA frustrated me, all of which added up to a feeling that I didn't fit in the program. I sensed that not trusting myself was my biggest problem, though I didn't understand how to express this at the time. I also found the idea of admitting powerlessness confusing, because that was all I ever felt: powerless. I could do powerlessness in my sleep. It was empowerment I craved. I left counselor number four's office feeling hopeless and defeated.

I was twenty-eight years old then, in 1996, and living alone in a bleak one-bedroom garden-level apartment in Parkville, Missouri. Fresh from another painful breakup, I had a working theory of why my life wasn't working. I couldn't drink without overdrinking, no matter how hard I tried. I'd been addicted to alcohol for years, and the foundation of self-loathing beneath me was made up of every broken promise I'd made to myself to stop.

One gray November day several weeks after that therapy appointment, I found myself back in the self-help section of a bookstore. This was long before Google offered tons of information about personal matters for people to access in the privacy of their own homes, so I had to rely on bookstores and libraries. Over the years, I'd read just about every book I could find on the subject of addiction recovery. Recovery memoirs helped me feel less alone, but the endings were always the same . . . *And then I went to meetings and worked a twelve-step program for the rest of my life.* I feared I was one of the "unfortunates" from AA literature:

> Those who do not recover are people who cannot or will not completely give themselves to this simple program, usually men and women who are constitutionally incapable of being honest with themselves. There are such unfortunates.

Desperate for another way out, I continued my search. The back cover of a book titled *Rational Recovery,* by Jack Trimpey, grabbed my attention:

> AVRT (Addictive Voice Recognition Technique) is an aggressive self-recovery program that shows you exactly how to take control of your addictive behavior now—and how to recover totally through planned abstinence.

New book in hand, I raced to my apartment, filled
with hope, sensing this approach might be the one.
I plopped down on my dingy sofa and read hungrily,
desperate for the promised enlightenment. Within
minutes, I knew it had arrived. The words instantly
made sense to me. The author described a disconnection that some people, like me, feel with the
recovery-group solution, and his words validated my
suspicion that there must be more than one path to
sobriety, that there was surely another method that
others had used effectively for years.

> Addictive Voice Recognition Tech-
> nique (AVRT) is the name Rational
> Recovery has given to a very simple
> thinking skill that permits anyone
> to recover immediately and com-
> pletely from addiction to alcohol or
> drugs. AVRT is also a description of
> how human beings naturally recover
> from substance abuse, alcohol or drug
> dependence, or "addiction." For eons,
> people have been figuring out AVRT
> on their own, but they have not named
> it. This special knowledge has been
> around for as long as people have felt
> the sting of substance pleasure, yet

it has never been set down as educational material.[1]

I read, absorbed, and allowed the words to reach me. Rational Recovery, I learned, was not a program to be followed but a process to be learned. Trimpey's simple message, which I had heard nowhere else but somehow knew in my bones, was that permanent abstinence is achieved by forcing something out of hiding and dealing with it directly. He named this hiding thing the Addictive Voice. "The Addictive Voice is the *only* reason you drink," he wrote.

I was on board immediately. Total freedom was possible but required critical awareness and full accountability. Most important, I had to learn how to trust myself completely. This was the piece I had longed for but until now hadn't been able to find. It felt like a path back to a former, stronger version of myself. Hope flooded through me, and I felt awake again. Alive.

The book explained that there were two coexisting sides of my mind that were causing my constant inner battle: the side that wanted to keep drinking and the side that didn't. This was new to me.

---

1. Jack Trimpey, *Rational Recovery: The New Cure for Substance Addiction* (New York: Pocket Books, 1996), 29.

The voice of your addiction, the AV with its sentences, images, and feelings, is always with you, and it is your own worst enemy . . . It is an enemy within you that survives . . . in order to drink. It fears anything or anyone that would threaten its supply of that very precious stuff . . . It creates countless reasons to continue drinking. It remains disguised as you, operates in hiding from others who would interfere with your drinking . . .

On the one hand, *you* want to quit. On the other hand, "you" don't want to quit . . . These two *voices* argue endlessly . . .

Your goal is to become one—your own self, free from addiction and free to live as you choose.[2]

The author identified the difference between me and *It*. *It* is the voice of my addiction. I was relieved to find the focus of the book wasn't on the origin of the vice but on a solution for dealing with it. According to Trimpey, in order to maintain permanent abstinence, I would need to identify those times when *It*

---

2. Trimpey, *Rational Recovery: The New Cure for Substance Addiction*, 109.

pretends to be me, and when *It* tries to hijack my reasoning and convince me to drink despite all the consequences that would follow. But *It* was, by definition and name, *not me* and would never be me. *It* was only a voice in my head, a voice with one goal, one answer to every single question: drink.

In the book, a specific trick is suggested to prove who's in charge. As soon as I read it, I put the book down and went into my bedroom, sat on the edge of my bed, and concentrated. Holding my right hand out in front of me, I instructed *It*, the voice that just seconds ago was telling me to *put the stupid book down and get a drink like you know you will eventually anyway,* to move my fingers. My fingers didn't move. *It* told me and would continue to tell me many, many, many things. Allowed to rule, that voice could convince me of anything. But a voice alone couldn't move my hand by itself—*ever. It* was only a voice. *It* was ultimately powerless.

Then I instructed myself—the real me, the one in charge—to move my hand. I wiggled my fingers and screamed in delight. I got it! I understood the difference between me and *It*, the voice of my addiction pretending to be me. I understood the glorious power behind this simple concept. I could move my fingers any time I wanted, which meant I was also completely in charge of whether I moved them to pick up a drink or not. That not-me voice—the one that told me drinking was good, always, and that showed no regard for my health, dreams, family, or future—could not. I still remember the joy I felt that day as I sat on the edge of my bed.

To a person who's never been addicted, my excitement about learning to separate these voices may sound ridiculous. But addiction emerges slowly, like any other abusive relationship. The abuser never strikes on the first date. There's a grooming process, a wearing down of one's free will. Soon you find yourself serving a master that wins your loyalty by providing intense pleasure, or temporary relief from pain, or both. That's what had happened to me. The combination of intense pleasure and temporary relief from pain had made life bearable when I felt unable to make it so otherwise. I'd been serving that master for years.

Once I was back in charge of my own mind—a position I'd lost after addiction took hold—hope returned, and hope changed everything. What followed were six of the most glorious weeks of my life, weeks filled with joy, even though nothing else in my life had changed. I practiced my new trick each time *It* brought to mind images of frosty glasses of beer, promised me ecstasy via ice-filled tumblers, or asked me *It*'s all-time favorite question: *Why not have a drink now, when you know you will later?* Each time, I held my right hand in front of my face and said to *It*, "If you can move my fingers, I'll take you to the liquor store." I stared at my unmoving hand and smiled. Sometimes I said out loud, "That's what I thought, motherfucker."

One afternoon in early 1997, six weeks after my moment of revelation on my bed, I was at a movie theater with a friend watching *The First Wives Club* when *It* snuck up on me again. In one scene, Goldie Hawn drinks a cocktail while walking on a treadmill. The image struck me, and something inside began to salivate.

> *It*: *You could stop by the liquor store after the movie.*

> Me: *Wait. I don't drink anymore. Stop. I see you.*

I went back to watching the movie, feeling the familiar rush of peace in my ability to identify the voice of my addiction. In another scene, Goldie's friends confront her about her drinking and toss all her liquor bottles in the trash. So many bottles flying, crashing. An unsettled feeling came over me, a nervousness. *It* pounced.

> *It*: *A drink would be so amazing after being abstinent for so long.*

Me: *No. I feel wonderful. I'm finally free! I'm excited to go home and make something healthy to eat.*

It: *Yes, of course. And wine would be good with that . . .*

Me: *Stop. Screw you. Rational Recovery taught me that I don't have to listen to this.*

It: *Sure. You know that's all a crock, right? I mean, no counselor ever recommended this method even once. Every book you've read, every person you've met says no one can do this without AA. You know you're going to end up there in the end. Everybody does. In fact, if you think about it, having some drinks today will help you accept real recovery tomorrow. The sooner you prove this false recovery isn't possible, the sooner you can get sober for good.*

Me: *But I've been feeling so good.*

It: *Have I? I've been a little lonely and bored. If this is all there is to life, what's*

the point? I might as well have some
fun. No one will know anyway.

The book had warned me. The voice of my addiction's slickest maneuver is hijacking the pronouns in my head. *It* changed *you* into *I* and hid from me. My pronoun mistake ended my six weeks of sweet freedom. I bought a bottle of Jack Daniel's on the way home and plunged back into the darkness, where I remained for another decade.

I slunk back to AA, convinced I'd fallen for a trick, a false promise that led me astray, but my dilemma remained the same. Despite my committed efforts and the wonderful people in the meetings, I never connected with the twelve-step program in a way that helped me stop for good.

Many years later, after I found freedom from alcohol, I wondered how my life might've been different if I'd trusted myself back then and returned to Rational Recovery after that day in the theater. But I see now that, for me, even with Rational Recovery there was still a critical missing piece. While the approach offered was spot-on for me in many ways, I hadn't yet addressed the pain and disconnection that led to my overuse of alcohol as an escape in the first place. I had no new coping skills for dealing with my thoughts and emotions. While AA does provide a place for alcoholics to learn new ways of living, I didn't find its environment helpful in that way when I was a young woman.

For so many reasons, individual therapy was a better place for me to do that work. I had very little money in my twenties and thirties, but I found free or low-cost options in the community. Allowing an objective, safe person into my inner world helped me see that I was wrong about so much—what I believed about myself, what I needed and didn't need, how to navigate the world as a sensitive and introverted woman, how to accept myself.

I returned to Rational Recovery years later, when I was ready. When I did, I found that while I'd been wrong about a lot, I'd been right about some things, too.

PERSONAL REFLECTION QUESTIONS

1. Share about a time in early adulthood when a book you read or a teacher you had changed the way you thought about yourself or the possibilities for your life.
2. What challenge or experience was most difficult for you in early adulthood, and which resources helped you to cope with it?
3. What are you most proud of about your early adulthood self?
4. Write an encouraging letter to your twentysomething self.
5. What beliefs do you hold about the idea of trusting yourself?

CHAPTER THREE

Rescue

The dry mountain air is a razor in my throat. Tomorrow I'll learn that I have strep throat, but on the side of this mountain today, I'm convinced it's a summer cold, and I berate myself for not being tougher. To make matters worse, something seems to be wrong with my right foot, and I'm starting to limp. I take off my backpack, unzip it, pull out two more Advil, and down them with the last bit of warm water from my green plastic sports bottle. My raw throat closes in protest. The four ibuprofen pills I took thirty minutes ago have not made a dent in the pain, and I'm not hopeful that these capsules will help, either, but I'm an addict, and to an addict more is always better.

Eagle Cliff Mountain sits by itself on the outer edge of Colorado's Rocky Mountain National Park, away from the summer crowds. My superfit older sister Jessie and her laid-back husband, Patrick, have hiked this trail before and want to show their preteen daughters the stunning view at the summit. Too prideful to stay back at the cabin, I'd told myself, *I'm going to feel crappy anyway. I may as well feel crappy in some beautiful scenery.*

I've made a terrible mistake.

I scope out a small groove between two boulders, lower myself to a leaning position, and try to catch my breath. My fever is masked by the heat of exertion. I've been ignoring my body's signals for years, but the pain in my right big toe now, combined with the pain in my throat, is pushing past my tolerance threshold. I hesitate to take off my beat-up Reeboks to investigate, afraid of the mangled mess I imagine lies beneath.

I carefully remove my right shoe and am shocked to see only my dirty white sock. No blood. My toenail is dying, but I don't know this at the time, and through my sock I can't see any evidence of such a development. The *subungual hematoma*, two words I learn in the doctor's office later, is causing blood to pool beneath the nail bed as my toe is repeatedly jammed against my ill-fitting tennis shoe. I can handle the excruciating pain, but the invisibility of it defeats me.

I lean back and watch the girls, Jade and Olivia, ease past me. They climb, bent over, their fit young arms and legs pushing, pulling. In a feverish flash of memory, I'm eleven again. It's field day on the playground at Minneha Elementary in late May 1980. The unrelenting, sunny Kansas heat beats down on the asphalt, and I'm sweating in my yellow polo shirt and jean shorts. My grandmotherly sixth-grade teacher, Mrs. Orsman, is posted by the pull-up bars, along with a volunteer parent, counting how many pull-ups each child can do in a minute. When it's my turn, I'm excited to give it a go.

I love field day. As a shy, slightly chubby bookworm of a girl, I am surprised by this fact. Recess and PE—unstructured, chaotic, and loosely monitored— are a nightmare for this socially anxious introvert. Large bullying boys turn those "fun" times into the most terrifying part of the day for those of us with no competitive thirst.

Girls and boys like me are the targets of loud, humiliating pronouncements of disgust if we make a misstep during a kickball or softball game. God forbid we miss a catch in the outfield or kick the ball weakly. Jared Miller and Shaun Hartley verbally harass any loser who costs their team a point. Sometimes that loser is me.

But field day is a bully-free zone where all the teachers and lots of parents help. A palpable spirit of camaraderie and celebration surround the entire event, which features relay races, pull-up stations, tug-of-war, and silky blue ribbons. The bullies are conspicuously silent today. Apparently, grade-school boys aren't quite so tough when Mom is watching. Free from the threat of being publicly shamed by the boys I secretly want to like me, I unleash my inner athlete. I am competitive after all, and I surprise everyone with my hidden strength.

"Sherry, I had no idea you were so athletic!" Mrs. Orsman exclaims as I pull my chin up and over the hot metal bar again and again.

◆ ◆ ◆

My toe throbs and I'm once again back in my unfit, middle-aged body. I look up and see only the side of an enormous boulder—flat, unyielding gray rock with no handholds to grab to pull myself up, even if I had the strength. I look down at a mile-long stretch of loose rock and jagged tree branches, a vertical decent I can't fathom. The pressure on my right foot will be unbearable going down. There's nowhere to go from here. My defenses falter, and the tears burst through.

Someone will have to call a helicopter. Keanu Reeves from Speed *will drop down holding on to a rope with one hand, a stretcher for me in the other, arm muscles bulging. All business—confident, brave, purposeful—he'll lose focus briefly as we lock eyes. Our undeniable sexual chemistry must be temporarily contained while he transports me to safety . . .*

"Look, we can see our cabin!" Jade's sweet voice interrupts as she marvels at the glorious scene from the top of the mountain, about fifty feet above me.

The others can't see me, so I let the tears stream down my face quietly. Every part of me aches. At thirty-seven, with one bad marriage and a string of destructive relationships behind me, I'm as unsure of who I am or what I want from life as I was at twenty. The one thing I excel at is suppressing pain, and now I'm failing at that, too.

How did this happen to me? What am I running from?

It occurs to me then that I'm not running *from* anything. I'm chasing. I am trying to find my way inside of something but have only managed to get further away. The memory of the glorious feeling I've been trying to recapture all these years floods my brain.

♦ ♦ ♦

"Oooo, lookee here at what wanted to come out and play." Eva leaned back against the closet door and smiled as she pulled the large brown bottle from her overnight bag.

It was the fall of 1982, and I was thirteen, sitting cross-legged on the floor between Katherine Jenkins's bed and closet. Five girls sat in a circle, two of them exceptionally cool. Eva and Katherine went way back, their families connected by wealthy social circles my parents didn't even know existed. While I'd spent the past few years mowing lawns and babysitting for a bit of cash, these two had been learning about Borghese makeup, *Vogue* magazine, and Calvin Klein.

A friend of mine since elementary school, Katherine had an elegant sophistication that had been lost on the rest of us until her "cool factor" skyrocketed at age thirteen. Her proudly extravagant socialite mother helped Katherine throw amazing parties. Invitations written in Katherine's messy scrawl were a golden ticket to popularity when we were in middle school. Her frequent companion, Eva, a beauty of Armenian ancestry with miles of thick black curls, was a born leader of girls. All five of us sitting in the room that October night were smart and did well in school, but Eva's sharp intelligence and irreverent wit tended to incite either strong feelings of admiration or terrified disdain. I was firmly planted in the first camp.

"What'd you bring? Vodka?" Katherine asked. She was apparently a pro at distinguishing types of alcohol. I knew only two categories: beer and liquor.

"No, no, dearest. Vodka is for the mild-mannered mommies. Allow me to introduce you to Mr. Scotch, the preferred beverage of real men like us." Eva looked us each in the eye as she unscrewed the lid ceremoniously. "The question is . . . who is the manliest among us?"

"I'll go." I reached for the bottle.

My motivation was simple: I needed whatever magic potion they were ingesting that made them so much stronger than me. An eager student, I wanted to learn how to morph from a frustrated girl-child into a powerful, seductive sorceress. In my own body, I felt the barely suppressed feminine aggression I'd witnessed emanating from them. I'd found my tribe at last. And yet, I secretly feared that there was a difference between them and me and that I'd forever remain outside the group, watching.

I put the bottle to my lips and took a hefty swig before passing it on. The offensive medicinal bite of the first burning gulp was a long-lost memory by the time the bottle made its way back to me. I leaned back on the bed frame as a warm glow melted away the walls. I looked around the group and smiled. I was finally inside.

That is my last memory from the night, though tales of me spinning around like a madwoman—and nearly busting through a wall of windows—served as inside-joke material for years.

I chased that feeling, that moment when the scotch had hit my bloodstream and my vigilant inner guard dogs went off duty, for more than two decades. In high school I chased it with strawberry wine coolers, horrific and high-octane orange MD "Mad Dog" 20/20, and the Jack Daniel's we swiped from Eva's mom's stash—whatever I could get my hands on. After high school, I continued the chase with cheap white wine or Southern Comfort straight from the bottle. In my twenties, I chased that feeling in bars, with Bacardi and Diet Coke. I spent several more years chasing it with cheap chardonnay before I met vodka and fell in love.

My friends all drank, too. But somehow, I failed to ever locate the elusive stop button other people pushed by eating something or going to sleep or, incredibly, switching to water after a few drinks. Those annoying aliens were to be avoided, but there were plenty of people like me. We found each other easily and continued the chase side by side. I was a good girl from a good family, and I became a good alcoholic, too, quietly drinking myself to a sort of living death. Nobody knew the extent of my problem.

At the time I found myself on the side of the mountain—injured and exhausted, rounding the corner into middle age—a part of me was still thirteen, sitting on that bedroom floor with the impossibly cool girls, longing to feel as beautiful and powerful as I thought they were. To be safely enfolded into the circle of the gang. The truth was that I hadn't felt much of anything for years. The last time I remembered crying was on the phone with Eva six years before this day, and eighteen years after we'd sat on Katherine's floor passing that bottle around. She was the first person I told when Dominic left me six months into our marriage.

I'd married Dominic in the fall of 1999 when I was thirty, supposedly old enough to choose wisely. The following March, I sat alone in the overpriced, gloomy Kansas City two-bedroom apartment we'd both hated. For three days, I sat motionless in his beloved black leather La-Z-Boy recliner emblazoned with the Seattle Seahawks logo. He was obsessed with the team, and the chair was his prized possession, a security object that I pictured cradling him like an enormous hand. This prompted me to refer to it as "The Hand" in a private joke with my sister. When Dominic left me, I was more surprised that he'd been willing to leave that damn chair.

As I sat in the detestable chair, I replayed one moment over and over in my head.

"I think we should separate." I'd said these words as I stood next to The Hand, looking down at the man I still wanted but didn't know how to reach, desperate for a fight. Starting a fight was all I had left. There was almost nothing between us anymore. I knew he'd been unfaithful, but I felt like the idiot for marrying a man who'd cheated on me even before we were married. I often thought to myself after it became clear that divorce was imminent that I'd somehow married the only man in the world that I knew *for sure* would cheat on me.

He looked away from the television long enough to level me with a hateful stare, his brown eyes turning dark. Then silence. This was his best strategy for avoiding another fruitless argument. No, actually, I take that back. His best strategy was what he did the next day.

The day after the fight that wasn't a fight, I noticed he was a half hour late coming home from work. Then an hour. Three hours. Ten hours. At fourteen hours, my anxious anger turned to shock, and I entered a frozen state as the reality of his abandonment sank in. I sat in his chair and I waited. By twenty-four hours, movement was difficult, the air around me cement. Using the remote required focused effort.

TV on, off, on, off. Thirty-six hours. Lights on, off, on, off. Forty-eight hours. No sleep, no food, no drink, no feeling. Seventy-two hours.

I imagined taking a butcher knife to the back cushion of the hideous chair, exposing what I imagined to be a still, black heart behind that cruel-looking blue bird with its deadly hooked beak. The Hand had been my enemy all along, with its smug promise to forever remain a one-seater, protecting whoever sat in it to watch TV from ever having to accidentally touch another person.

"What do you mean he's *gone*?" Eva's shocked voice came through the phone.

It had been months since I'd spoken to her. We lived in separate cities, different worlds. It seemed to me that I was always chasing her, and sometimes I got tired and stopped. Time would pass until I broke down and called, which, until the phone rang that day, I'd forgotten I'd done the day before.

I hadn't even invited her to the wedding, a tiny ceremony at my sister's home in Lenexa, Kansas. My father had given me a thousand dollars for the whole affair, and I came in well under budget. My sweet ivory sleeveless dress cost twenty-five dollars at a secondhand dress shop; alterations were another twenty-five. I loved the simplicity of my wedding, but mostly I'd wanted to get to the other side of it. I was lost. Marriage, I believed at the time, would solve everything.

Dominic had seemed like a departure from my old pattern, so I grossly misinterpreted our dynamic as healthy. It was true that he didn't need me in the claustrophobic way that my last serious boyfriend, Richard, had. Richard, whose brand of suffocating love I'd narrowly escaped several years back, had made Dominic seem safe by comparison. I was relieved to not feel responsible for Dominic's feelings. In fact, I had a difficult time even finding any of his feelings aside from his sexual feelings, which he had no problem accessing. After we got married, however, I began to see that I'd overcorrected and ended up with a man so emotionally disengaged that I found myself looking up the definition of *sociopath* a lot. I had mistaken his remoteness for respect. Once again, I was in a relationship that had the same defining characteristic as the one I'd had with Richard: profound loneliness.

"I mean he didn't come home from work three days ago and he doesn't answer his phone." I leaned back and pulled the lever on the enormous chair, engaging the footrest. The sound of Eva's familiar voice and the relief I felt at finally saying the truth out loud had loosened my stiff joints after being nearly immobile for days.

I sucked in air hard. *Have I been breathing?* Eva had never met Dominic, and this wasn't the best introduction, but I was beyond caring whether she liked him or not. I had married out of a desperate need to fix all the broken parts of myself, but instead of providing a solution, my misguided decision had only added to my pile of failures. Neither Dominic nor I had the maturity or emotional health to navigate a committed relationship. My sham of a marriage was over. The jig was up.

"Oh, Eva." I wanted to cry but no tears came. "He was cheating the whole time with some skanky girl from work, and he didn't even care that I knew. The whole thing has been a nightmare."

"God, I am so sorry." The warmth in her voice pressed a button in me and the tears came.

"The worst part is, I've become a monster. I don't recognize myself anymore. He'd crawl into bed at six in the morning like it was nothing. I'd get so pissed I'd hit him sometimes—beat on his chest, screaming crazy shit at him like I was possessed. I totally lost it. Then every time I'd lose it, he'd look at me like I was insane. I totally get how murder happens."

"Sherry Lynn, now you listen to me." Eva's commanding voice broke through my haze. I was transported back to a familiar place of sanity and certainty. "Don't you dare forget *who you are*."

Her last three words were what finally got me out of the chair. I held on to them for days as I packed, made calls, did the practical work of moving forward. Not because *I* remembered who I was yet, but because she did.

• • •

"Sher, you're so close! You've got to see this!" I hear my sister Jessie's voice from a short distance ahead, where the winners at life are basking in their achievement. Perhaps sensing that I'm contemplating heading back down the mountain before reaching the top, she adds, "Come on!"

A firm but gentle command. Something in her voice tells me declining is not an option. For my indomitable sister, crying on the edge of a mountain, fifty feet from the top, is never an option.

My voice is gone. I'm unable to yell up to her and explain that I can't make it. I sense that she's coming to check on me, so I quickly wipe my face with my sweaty blue T-shirt.

Jessie peers over the edge of the boulder, spots me, and points out a groove several feet to my right, where a small but sturdy dead branch is poking out. "We came this way. Just put your foot there and grab on to that branch. After that it's easy. You're so close!"

Her clarity and her confidence in my ability penetrate my dark cloud. I notice that the release of tears has left something behind—an unexpected lightness, a tiny bit of relief. No helicopter is coming. Since my sister thinks I can make it, I'll try. I force myself to stand, promising my foot I'll take care of it soon if it'll just hold me up a little longer, and I follow my sister's directions.

I reach out and pull myself up.

PERSONAL REFLECTION QUESTIONS

1. Share about a time you longed to be rescued from yourself or some part of your life.
2. What do you think now about that desire to be rescued?
3. Has there been a time when you were "rescued" but the outcome wasn't what you'd hoped?
4. Who in your past has come to your rescue by believing in you? How did that impact your life?
5. When have you been the voice of rescue for someone else?
6. When have you been the voice of rescue for yourself?

CHAPTER FOUR

Visited

I'm sitting across from my niece Olivia, who's nineteen and almost unbearably beautiful. The crisp blue eyes staring back at me are the eyes of my father and sister, but Olivia's are accentuated with thick black liner—a look she can pull off without looking cheap because nothing she does with makeup, and she does a lot, ever distracts from her cherubic, perfectly symmetrical face with its tiny button of a mouth. Today her hair is platinum blond, cut short and spiky. She looks like a mix between a blond Katy Perry and Madonna in her video for "Papa Don't Preach."

Olivia is talking about her last drinking binge and subsequent blackout. The contrast between her whisper-soft voice and the tragically painful words coming out of her mouth boggles my mind a bit. Her irresistible, unguarded fragility brings Marilyn Monroe to mind in a way that alarms me. *How will she ever survive in this world?*

We're nestled into a cracked red-leather booth at Snowball, an old-fashioned ice-cream shop in the remote town of Atchison, Kansas, an hour from the suburbs of Kansas City where we both live. Framed prints of Marilyn and other dead cultural icons line the walls of the '50s-themed shop, tragic figures warning us from early graves. When we'd first walked in, my niece had pulled out her phone and snapped pictures of them. First and foremost, Olivia is an artist.

Atchison is known primarily for three things: Benedictine College, ghost tours of historic homes that are rumored to be haunted, and Valley Hope, the drug and alcohol rehabilitation center. Olivia checked herself in to Valley Hope two weeks ago after a particularly scary binge on the alcohol and drugs she has been abusing for several years. She's been given a pass to go out with me for the afternoon. Eleven years ago, almost to the day, I checked out of the same rehab.

"Sorry I was frustrated earlier," Olivia says. "That nurse is such a pain. She can never just give me my meds without spending an hour checking to see if I can have them. I mean, I know she's just doing her job but . . ."

Olivia's attention-grabbing appearance is at odds with her shy nature. She is typically quiet, a natural observer like me, so the fact that she is talking nonstop now leaves me stunned and disoriented, as if I'm meeting her for the first time. When I picked her up, she was talking the reluctant nurse into giving her a Ritalin tablet, for which she has a legitimate prescription to treat her nearly debilitating ADHD. I can tell by the near-manic pace at which she's talking that she won the battle.

"That's OK," I manage to get out before she jumps into a riveting one-sided dialogue about the events of the past few weeks that led to her rehab stay.

"So you remember Katie? Well, she overdosed again and that scared me because she, like, almost *died*, and then I had that terrible night—the one I was telling you about, remember? And I was so sick and scared and, like, didn't know what else to do, so I decided to try this place, but I hated it at first, *hated* it, but now I am, like, I don't know . . . people notice things about me that I forgot, you know? And I am, like, *awake* again, you know? And so . . ."

She leaves no conversational gap into which I might step and ask a pertinent question or impart some great nugget of wisdom. I am relieved because it is all I can do just to concentrate on keeping my jaw from hitting the table. I do a lot of nodding. Yes. I know. I know exactly.

I'm in two places simultaneously—actively forcing myself to stay present and not miss a moment of being invited into Olivia's experience and also feeling as though I'm with my former self, eleven years ago: a thirty-eight-year-old in 2006, sitting at this same ice-cream shop, allowing someone else into *my* experience. *Did we sit in this exact same booth?*

Now she's talking about the nice guy she met, the thirty-four-year-old heroin addict. I don't tell her about the nice guy I met when I was in rehab, too—the one sitting beside her in the booth now, whose ghost I've been staring at the whole time she's been talking.

• • •

Andy was ugly-sexy. Others probably thought he was just ugly, but that had more to do with his personality than his looks. He was the kind of man other men hated on sight and self-respecting women steered clear of by avoiding eye contact and not encouraging his obnoxiousness. Back then, that kind of overly confident, abrasive, aggressive, and mean exterior was like catnip for me.

His forearms caught my eye first. I noticed one day that they seemed impressively masculine—large, muscular, and exceptionally well formed. Before then, I'd been aware of him in the way that we patients were all aware of each other—comrades and equals in a place where we all were addicts. I knew he was about my age and was going through a divorce.

One day about two weeks in, we were all sitting in a circle—there is a lot of circling up in rehab—and he was draped across a chair that he'd turned backward, in the way that large, domineering men sometimes do. Suddenly I became aware of him in a new way, as more than six feet of lean, tattooed, tan, man body clad in extremely well-fitting Levi's.

Though everything about his demeanor seemed hard and angry, his bright eyes twinkled with intelligence and his dirty-blond hair looked soft and touchable. The contrast appeared to be a problem he was trying to overcome by being loud and overbearing, hiding his pent-up rage behind the guise of helpful confrontation. He'd shout, "Bullshit!" in a booming voice if a fellow addict dared to share something that didn't ring true on his authenticity meter, which was as unreliable as all his other meters, from what I could tell.

I was surprised by my reaction to those forearms, nearly forgetting they were attached to a whole man. He caught me staring, and I held his intense green-eyed gaze.

In that first millisecond when I didn't look away, I saw him transform from just another circled-up inmate drone into something alive with animal sexual energy invisible to everyone but me. Holding his gaze several seconds too long, I didn't smile coyly—I didn't smile at all. Casually and slowly, I looked back at the speaker, deeply satisfied that I'd ignited in someone a spark I hadn't realized I could still ignite. I felt him staring at me for the rest of the meeting, but I didn't look back.

Patients aren't left alone much in rehab, so after the initial spark, we shared several delicious days of long looks across sterile rooms and secret, daring knee touches under cracked Formica cafeteria tables, and even a bold moment of watching TV in the communal living room when I let my forearm brush against his, sending an electric charge tearing through my body. Then finally, we had our moment.

One evening after dinner, six of us gathered in an alcove at the bottom of the stairs where a small table covered with colorful paints and markers triggered vague memories of classroom artistic humiliations that had left me craft phobic. Andy and I waited for the conversation to die out, for each person to say good night and head for bed, leaving us alone for the first time.

The door hadn't fully closed on the last person to leave when he turned to me from where he again sat on a metal folding chair turned backward, looked into my eyes, and stated as if he'd been dying to say it for days, "You are so beautiful."

A direct hit. I was ashamed of how desperately I'd wanted to hear those words from a man, but I was unable to deny the depth of the need. It had been years since someone looked at me with such intensity, since I'd felt enchanting, desired. I hadn't realized I was starving until he handed me a steak. Too overwhelmed to respond, I smiled and said nothing. The deal was sealed.

He told me later that he regretted not kissing me that night, but it was one of the rare times he read a social situation correctly. I would've been turned off by the premature advance. For me, the pleasure was in the prolonged dance, the forbidden nature of the connection, the buildup of sexual tension.

Of course, we patients had been warned about, even outright prohibited from, engaging in romantic relationships. Apparently, getting caught up in a new relationship with someone equally life challenged was a bad idea that could distract us from the deep inner work we were there to do. Like a true addict, I understood that these warnings were directed toward everyone but me.

Like many functioning alcoholics, I'd managed to acquire a college degree, and I had a nice apartment, a stable job, a reliable car, and supportive family and friends. Andy had a soon-to-be ex-wife, debt, multiple DUIs, and a manipulative father who wanted his drinking buddy back. None of this mattered to me. By the time we left Valley Hope, we were in love.

His physique was pretty close to perfect. I remember one particular day in my apartment when we were fresh out of rehab and grappling with early sobriety. I'd only known him a matter of weeks, but we were inseparable, desperately clinging to each other in this terrifying exposed state in which we found ourselves, our masks and shields stripped away.

He was sprawled facedown across my bed wearing only jeans, his arms spread out and his hands improbably touching both sides of the king-size bed, tattoos etched across tanned skin over powerful muscles. The breathtaking image of him in this position burned into my psyche. I let my physical attraction to him override my need for a relationship with depth and sanity for far longer than I now like to admit.

I was turned on at the time but had no idea how to engage and relate without the liquid courage I'd relied upon for so many years. I'm guessing it was the same for him. For such a highly sexually charged relationship, however, there was very little actual sex happening. Acting sexual was something we had down, but engaging in true intimacy was an entirely different proposition. We were emotional children in adult bodies.

I relapsed first. It happened on a rare evening when we were apart. The snake of temptation whispered familiar promises, and I fell for them. I zipped over to the liquor store and bought my standard enormous bottle of cheap white wine, ceremoniously poured the first glass, and savored every millisecond of the well-practiced ritual. As the electric sensation eased its way from my belly to my extremities, I returned to the deepest center of myself. My whole body sighed. *Ah, home again.*

I awoke alone on a rough sofa with only a fuzzy recollection of how I'd gotten there. I remembered that some people and I had formed a group, in the way that drunken strangers do, at the bar I'd gone to after polishing off the wine. We had caravanned to a young man's house after the bar closed. Our odd group of instant buddies included a woman I knew vaguely through work and several geeky guys who were about ten years younger than us.

I came to with a familiar sense of dread and quickly assessed the damage in the way that alcoholics do: *Is my body intact? Where's my purse?* My relief was predictably followed by a desperation to get home and enter the next phase in the cycle: being grateful for having lived through another visit to the dark side and feeling certain this nightmare would be the final lesson I needed before getting clean for good.

I called Andy at six o'clock in the morning to come pick me up. I knew without him telling me that he'd been on the reverse side of this drive of shame many times in his life. In the end, we didn't talk about it much. He was less concerned with my relapse than he was with what I had or hadn't done with the men from the bar. I didn't waste much effort on trying to convince him of my innocence. We both knew exactly how these things went, the fuzziness of the details. The possible romantic betrayal was a surface issue anyway, because alcohol was our one true love.

He relapsed several days later, and shortly after that we began drinking together. The relationship devolved predictably and immediately. The reasons for that warning we'd received in rehab became crystal clear to me, but that awareness came too late.

For the first time in years, I had a partner in my love-hate relationship with booze. At first, I thought maybe the arrangement could work—an exciting threesome. Instead, Andy quickly became a walking manifestation of everything I hated about myself. Back under the spell of alcohol, my once socially awkward new boyfriend was now arrogant, avoidant, indulgent, irresponsible, selfish, immature, out of control, and slightly insane.

When we were trying to be sober together—which was always my idea after another blurry night of fighting that ended with me locked in the bathroom crying—his weakness and inevitable failure seemed intolerable and disgusting to me. When he drank, I self-righteously tore into him or, worse, iced him out. But when I was the one who couldn't keep the promise, which was about half of the time, I resented him for standing between me and my drink.

When we drank together, instead of bonding and having fun like I'd had with friends from my past, we turned on each other and became dangerous enemies. He morphed into a hyperextroverted version of himself, one I was quick to identify as a male chauvinist pig.

"Put on Hank Williams Jr.," he drawled as if he were from the Deep South.

"Oh my God. Please. No." I physically blocked him from the CD collection and turned up the Indigo Girls.

I went the opposite direction when I drank, going deeper inside myself. I preferred either to be left alone with my music or to engage in intense, pseudointellectual conversation on deep topics. He was quick to identify this version of me as a condescending bitch. The drinking versions of ourselves demonstrated how incredibly mismatched we were as a couple and exacerbated those differences. This frustrated us both and ruined the fun times we'd imagined our shared love of drinking promised us.

A long breakup/make-up roller coaster began— short periods of strained sobriety during which we tried to be our best selves and support each other, followed by failed attempts to have fun together in the only way we knew how: drinking. This, of course, didn't work and ruined the single pleasure we each counted on in life.

It was a dismal situation that neither of us had any idea how to fix. I pushed him away whenever I felt overwhelmed or became afraid of him, two responses that increased in intensity over time, sensing that getting out of the relationship was the only answer for me. But he had no one else to turn to and nowhere else to go. I felt sorry for him, felt guilty and responsible, and agreed to help him as a friend, which inevitably led to more drinking together and more fighting.

We were playing the "just friends" game six months after rehab when I went to visit him at his new apartment in Bolivar, Missouri, where he'd moved to make a fresh start. We were buying food to make dinner on Halloween night when he told me a story that made me cry in the grocery store. It was the way he recounted the tale, as if it were a silly childhood memory, that nearly took me to my knees.

Andy's father had been a hard-core biker dude—a hard-living, hard-drinking man raising two kids in Kansas City part-time after multiple divorces, doing his best to toughen up his kindhearted only son. One Halloween, when Andy was about eight, he begged his dad to take him trick-or-treating. Deep into his nightly bottle of whiskey, his dad promised to take Andy if he first ran down the street to the store to buy some milk. Andy ran excitedly to the store and carried the plastic jug home as fast as he could. Just inside the house he tripped, spilling the milk all over the floor. His dad smacked him hard across the face and sent him to his room, where he stayed by himself the whole night, crying as he listened to the laughter of the neighborhood kids going door-to-door in their silly costumes.

Andy told me many stories about his life over the course of our time together. Most of them involved being hit, neglected, or emotionally tormented, though in his telling of it all, those aspects of the stories came across as incidental. I'm not sure why this one got to me more than the others. Maybe it was a cumulative effect, the result of hearing one more in a long line of such accounts, but when he got done telling me that story, my face was wet with tears. In front of the squash bin, we exchanged a look that remains locked in my memory. I saw what he'd felt his whole adult life—that he never had a fucking chance.

When I realized we were doomed as a couple, I tried and failed countless times to set healthy boundaries and extricate myself from our twisted connection. As I attempted this, he at one point declared with unintentionally hilarious sincerity, "But you can't leave me. I have a *perfect* body."

"Phhht!" My reaction was an involuntary head toss backward. The argument was so ridiculous that I couldn't even come up with a response. I left him

immediately—and about fifteen more times before the last time.

It became clear to me over time that while I had dreams to pursue, a life ahead of me that was worth living if only I could get myself together, he didn't have that same sense of hope for himself. No matter how hard I tried to help him see his potential, I couldn't make him see what I saw in him. He'd threaten suicide whenever I tried to leave him. And I would come running back to him, to reassure him and to try to convince him he had so much to live for even if we weren't together.

But I was increasingly aware of being in a trap—unable to take care of myself when I was with him, and unable to leave him for fear that he wouldn't make it without me. I tried to get him into therapy, even went with him to one session, but he went only because I pushed it. He downplayed his problems to the therapist—told the man he wasn't suicidal. Andy refused to go back to therapy, and finally, I refused to go back to him. I wished him well and cut off all communication, knowing it was the only way to disentangle myself from the futility of trying to save him when I was drowning myself.

I believe I would've held that final boundary, but I can't know for sure. Andy hung himself with a belt in his apartment and died five days before his fortieth birthday. He reached out to me one final time that day, but I didn't respond. I had put a hard stop to all communication with Andy a month before. I had a chance at a new life. I was ready to grab it and hold on tight, but I knew that doing this meant leaving him once and for all.

I had enrolled in graduate school and was pursuing my dream of becoming a therapist—a role I knew I couldn't fulfill in my current state. The part of me that fit with Andy was dying so that something new could be born. After his death, even though I believed deep down that I had done the right thing, the only thing I could have done to save my own life, it still took years for me to sort through the complicated feelings of loss, lingering questions about my own role and responsibility, and unfairness of all he endured in his life while I was able to recover and move forward.

I'll never understand that last part, but I did come to accept that it isn't mine to understand. I was eventually able to release the heaviness of the guilt I carried for not responding to his last call. I'd known when I ended the relationship for good that I was firing myself from the impossible job of keeping him safe from himself, of keeping him alive. I'd made peace with my decision in those weeks after we broke up, accepting the likelihood of a tragic ending to his story and my own powerlessness to stop him from spiraling out of control. But the reality of losing a person you love to suicide feels cruel in a way that never leaves you completely.

Andy's death and my own rebirth happened simultaneously, and the reasons for this are far beyond my human capacity to understand. What I did understand, though, and understand still, was that my job from that moment on was to honor the unearned gift that I'd received. In the days and weeks and months that followed, I allowed Andy's death to be the catalyst for my own transformation. I made him an integral part of a beautiful story about redemption and salvation. But in order to do this, I had to conquer my own demons.

My relationship with Andy and its tragic ending opened my eyes to the darker force hiding beneath my alcohol addiction—my dismal relationship with myself. I began to see that I had some learning to do about the difference between love and fear and the insidious nature of my need for control. I took responsibility for my misguided efforts to save Andy while I still wasn't yet well myself. I'd known the word *codependency* before all of this, but now I *understood* it. I began to realize that codependency—my tendency to sacrifice my own well-being to try to help someone else or remain in a relationship—was my core problem, which jump-started my focused study on the topic and my active recovery process.

When I received the somber message about Andy's death from his sister on my answering machine on that hot August day, I vowed that I'd never again stay in a relationship with someone out of a need to save him from himself or out of a need for him to save me from myself.

I'm so glad to be able to say that I've kept that promise.

• • •

Olivia and I leave Andy's ghost in the ice-cream shop and walk briskly to my Toyota RAV4 in the bitter cold. She asks if I'll stop at the Conoco and buy her a pack of cigarettes before we head back to Valley Hope. She is too young to buy them herself and has no money.

I'm her forty-eight-year-old aunt who has loved her since the day she was born. I'm a role model to her now, someone she can relate to because I too have struggled with addiction, and because we share layers of sameness that we're just starting to discover. I'm a mental health professional with a license that carries with it a heavy responsibility to do no harm. I'm a coach who leads trainings on healthy boundaries. I've built my new life and my professional work around the practice of identifying and countering manipulation and around helping people stay true to themselves when others try to control them. Am I going to buy cigarettes for my nineteen-year-old niece? Hell no.

"I'm sorry, but no. I can't do it." My reply is calm but firm.

We're bundled up in heavy coats as I navigate the empty, eerily familiar streets on this gray Saturday in late December.

"I'll just get them anyway," she declares, without the slightest hint of snark. She's a master manipulator, like all addicts—like I used to be—but her real superpower is her youthful ability to plainly state indisputable facts.

A bolt of panic races up from my belly, grips my heart, and lands at the base of my throat. *I must stop her from buying those cigarettes. I must stop her from falling in love with the heroin addict. I must stop her from ever drinking or using drugs again. I must stop her from destroying herself. I must stop her from living the life I lived, from feeling the pain I felt and caused others . . .*

But I'm at a complete loss—frozen, terrified. Have I learned nothing? Wait . . .

It comes to me then and the panic subsides, giving way to a strangely comforting feeling of resignation. I remember the promise I made to myself after Andy died. I remember what I've been telling others professionally for years now, the thing I believe, with all my being, to be true.

I can't stop her.

It's not within my power to stop her. The minute I start trying to stop her, start trying to control her, I will lose the ability to feel my love for her and to address her from a place of love instead of fear.

The reality is she gets to make her own choices just like Andy did. Just like I did. No one could stop me from buying cigarettes and drinking to excess and abandoning myself to toxic situations and people, and no one can stop her, either. She's free to choose, and I want her to be free. Watching her exercise this freedom is excruciating sometimes, but it's also an extraordinary experience. Because as familiar as this all is to me, Olivia is not me. Everything she does surprises me, and I don't want to miss a moment of it, even the parts that break my heart.

I have bucketloads of wisdom to impart when she's ready. I'll share everything I've learned along the way, support her on her own journey to loving herself and on whatever path to freedom from addiction she chooses. But this will all take time. I need to be patient.

In the meantime, I can set boundaries. As is often the case with boundaries, I can look back and wonder if I should've handled the situation differently, drawn a different line. And I can forgive myself for not doing it perfectly, because no one does.

Olivia smiles almost imperceptibly when I tell her, without a hint of resentment or exasperation, "We can stop at the gas station. But I won't buy them for you."

I smile, too. My fear is enormous, cavernous, bottomless. My love is so much bigger.

PERSONAL REFLECTION QUESTIONS

1. Have you ever felt responsible for keeping another adult safe from themselves, though you didn't really have the power to do so?

2. If a young person that you care about were traveling down the same difficult path you once traveled, what do you think would help them most?

3. Tell your own story, if you have one, of a codependent relationship from your life. What can you see now that you weren't able to see at the time?

4. If you're currently in a relationship with a person (intimate partner, parent, sibling, adult child) who's self-destructive or mentally ill, in what ways do you take care of yourself? Name five ways you're proud of yourself in your handling of this difficult circumstance.

5. How do you think people learn to love themselves?

6. Share about your experience with loving someone who doesn't have self-love.

CHAPTER FIVE

Loving Eva

The seats near gate fifty-seven at Denver International Airport are mostly empty. I choose one near an electrical outlet and plug in my phone. I'm headed to Los Angeles for ten days as part of the Master of Fine Arts in Creative Writing program I attend at Antioch University in Los Angeles.

The first time I took this trip to LA for school, in June 2017, I visited my therapist a month beforehand to practice techniques for managing my anxiety related to airports—not air*planes* but air*ports*. I'm directionally challenged and extremely introverted; large crowds and unfamiliar, hectic surroundings have always triggered my anxiety. But this midlife adventure has been about challenging fears and showing up fully in my life. No more hiding or avoiding. The prospect of conquering LAX and navigating LA by myself was one reason I chose a school so far from my home in Kansas. I thought if I forced myself to do this, I'd free myself from the travel anxieties that had built up over the years. I was right.

I pull out my iPad to check my messages and notice, with a tiny pinprick in my chest, the brown leather boots on the young woman sitting across from me. They're the color of milk chocolate, zipped up over her calves, with a high squared heel. I see boots on women all the time now, but each year certain styles inch closer to those worn in the late 1970s—closer to the look of the boots my sister Monica once owned. I get caught off guard each time I see a pair, but I don't typically allow the full memory to emerge. This time, however, with no pressing matters to divert my attention, I do.

I was nine the day Monica modeled her new boots in our living room. The oldest of three girls, she was, at thirteen, the first to show us how it happens, how a kid becomes something else entirely overnight.

"Come see. Mom took Monica shopping." My sister Jessie, eleven, poked her head in my room after knocking first. Despite the calm delivery, I could tell that she was sharing breaking news in her typically unflappable manner.

I looked up and replayed her words in my mind. *Wait. Mom took Monica shopping?*

Mom hated shopping. Her reason was that everything was too expensive. I hated shopping too, because the clothes at Sears were stiff and scratchy. Things never seemed to fit right.

I put my Hello Kitty bookmark in *Deenie,* the Judy Blume book I'd already read twice and followed Jessie down the narrow hallway. I knew that Dad was still at work, but I heard Mom and Monica talking in excited voices.

In the living room, I saw Monica strutting around, barely recognizable to me. She was wearing a fancy new outfit. Even her long brunette waves looked different somehow. I was spellbound by the way her new brown leather boots zipped up her calves and met the hem of her red-and-brown-plaid skirt. And those boots had *heels*—as high as the ones the younger teachers at school wore sometimes.

I glanced over at Mom, who never wore high heels herself and certainly never wore fancy boots, amazed that she was allowing this. Mom looked pleased. As we watched, my sister walked back and forth across the room, swirling and smiling. She looked beautiful, confident, grown-up. I felt a sense of awe, the word *teenager* running through my mind. I felt the same thrill I experienced while watching Charlie's Angels take down the bad guys on TV—a hint that an exciting possibility was in my future, a secret power having something to do with hair and makeup and heels. The boots seemed magical to me; I hadn't seen Monica look this happy in a long time.

The next day after school I couldn't wait to get home and hear about Monica's big day wearing her new clothes. I imagined her telling me stories about the other girls admiring her and boys thinking she was cute.

"See ya, Frizz Head!" Shaun Hartley called out from the open window of the bus as I stepped onto the street. A typical Shaun Hartley move. There was no stopping my hair on humid days like this one, when it grew bigger and puffier with each passing hour. I pretended not to hear him, pretended no one else heard him, and pretended I wasn't about to cry. I walked fast until the bus was out of sight, then ran the rest of the way to my house and up the driveway.

Once inside, I dropped my book bag next to the coatrack in the small entryway. Jessie arrived home after me each day, so I listened for a minute to hear where I might find Mom and Monica. No sounds coming from the kitchen. I headed down the hallway toward the back of the house. Monica's bedroom door was closed. As I approached, I heard her sobbing and the muffled sound of Mom soothing her. I quickly entered my bedroom across the hall, shut the door, and sat on my bed. My worn paperback was sitting on the bedside table. I opened it and found Deenie waiting for me right where I left her.

"Welcome to American Airlines. Flight 852 to Los Angeles will be boarding shortly."

The airport announcement startles me, and my body jerks slightly. The young woman has caught me staring at her footwear, so I nonchalantly shift my gaze back to my iPad, relieved to be back in the present. The scars from the years of bullying she endured at school remain, but Monica has healed in many ways. She never wore those brown leather boots again, though, and I may always feel a little ache when I see a similar pair. The day she modeled them was the last time I saw her truly believe she was beautiful.

• • •

"Want to go drive around?" Monica asks from just inside the doorway.

I put down my book and look at her from my bed.

At nineteen, she doesn't live with us anymore but comes over to do her laundry sometimes. She's just under five feet two, three inches shorter than I am now at age fifteen. Her thick brown hair is pulled back into a long ponytail. I scan her face to take her emotional temperature. *Drive around* sometimes means "*Let's go hang out,*" and sometimes it's code for "*I'm going nuts and I need to talk.*"

When Monica got her driver's license several years back, our grandmother gave us her 1978 fire-engine-red Ford Granada. Since that day, Monica's favorite thing in the world to do has been to drive. I enjoy riding with her, so we've spent endless hours driving around the city on evenings and weekends. Sometimes we talk; sometimes we just listen to music on the radio.

It was on these drives that Monica had begun to share about the bullying she endured starting in middle school. One specific girl and her devoted followers destroyed Monica's spirit for sport—regularly humiliating and even physically attacking her in classrooms and in hallways and in bathrooms and on soccer fields. Though she would never tell me this directly, I suspect that the day she wore those boots, the day I thought she'd be a star, had been the worst day of all. She also told me on our drives about her depression. I knew back then that she was in therapy and on medication, but I wouldn't know, until she'd tell me in the car one day, that she had also been getting help for her suicidal thoughts.

The pile of homework I need to do crosses my mind, but I sense by the pinched look on Monica's face and the irritated tone of her voice that this is an *I'm-going-nuts* moment.

The phone by my bed rings. I hear Jessie answer it in the kitchen and call back to me that Eva is on the phone for me.

"Sure," I say to Monica. "In about half an hour?"

After Monica shuts my bedroom door, I grab the receiver of my black rotary phone and settle back against the headboard on my twin bed, excited that Eva has called me.

"Hi!"

When there's no sound from the other end of the line, I know. Eva is overwhelmed again, trying to speak but unable to do so yet. I sit quietly and wait as the silence gives way to the sound of her crying. Eventually, a few intelligible words break through, and she shares the most recent chaotic situation from her unstable homelife. I feel unsure how to help her, just like I'm unsure how to help Monica, but I am spellbound by the intensity and urgency of their needs.

Looking back now, I don't recall a single detail of these calls from our teenage years, only that there were quite a few of them. The pain of living in her home with a flamboyant but unstable mother and an absent father was beyond my imagination. Eva cried and screamed and I listened and soothed. Eventually, without fail, we laughed. By the end of each call, she felt grateful and heard; I felt valued and seen.

I had so many worries—about Monica, about my parents not knowing how to help her, and about my growing fear that they couldn't help me, either. My inner world felt enormous and expansive, but the outer world overwhelmed and terrified me. I lived deep inside myself with all of the characters from my books and my dreams of escaping to a different life where I was beautiful and popular and not shy and weird. When Eva and Monica turned to me for emotional support and I was able to help by just listening, I felt engaged. I felt *necessary*.

◆ ◆ ◆

Eva and I had started out as enemies. I met her on the last day of September in 1980 at an all-girls skating party at my classmate Katherine Jenkins's house to celebrate Katherine's twelfth birthday. Eva was a family friend of Katherine's who attended another school, but at this party she was to some girls nothing but a curvy, raven-haired, wide-brown-eyed intruder. And by some girls, I mean my best friend, Andrea, and me, who liked to think we ruled the carefully constructed social order of sixth-grade girls at Minneha Elementary.

Andrea whispered in my ear and I laughed just as Eva caught my eye and shot me a vicious look. Maybe the whisper was about Eva and maybe it wasn't—I actually don't remember anymore—but that fact didn't matter. It was on. Before we knew what was happening, a preteen-girl war had broken out, and the party had divided into two enemy camps. The betrayal I felt was swift and sharp as a few girls from my class inexplicably chose Eva's side.

Eva skated up to me, pointed to my frizzy hair, and threw her head back in laughter—the tween-girl equivalent of tossing a live hand grenade. I was stunned and mortified, holding back tears as I allowed my comrades to rush me back to our post in Katherine's bedroom and bathe my emotional wounds with their indignant disgust. This girl Eva obviously didn't understand the rules of engagement. Girls were supposed to be mean only behind each other's backs, not to their faces. My friends and I talked about her for the rest of the night, huddled in our sleeping bags as we plotted our revenge until we fell asleep. The next day I managed to avoid interacting with Eva until our moms picked us up. I was relieved the ordeal was over.

Our paths crossed again when we both entered the same middle school. I was prepared to continue our slumber party standoff, but Eva caught me off guard. One day in Mrs. Patterson's seventh-grade history class, a friend handed me a mean-spirited drawing that mocked our somber older teacher's hairstyle. I stifled a guilty giggle, and Eva looked over at me from across the room. She grinned and motioned for me to pass the paper her way. Still a little afraid of her, I found the surprise invitation exciting and didn't hesitate. When she saw the picture she snorted, unafraid of getting us all in trouble. She passed the crude caricature back with a thought bubble added: *I'm never going back to Javier. He screws up my perm every time!* The tightness in my center loosened, and I laughed out loud, Eva's approval so important to me I couldn't give in to feeling bad about the joke.

The war was over. My former enemy turned out to be hilarious and intriguing, and she still played by a different set of rules than I had learned. I'd been raised to listen to adults, not question them. I was amazed that anyone, especially a girl, could be so bold. During class, Eva confidently challenged information or instructions if she didn't understand or agree. In the hallway between classes she modeled her eclectic outfits—flowing skirts with leggings, chunky jewelry, cool blazers over concert T-shirts—as if she were meeting up with Stevie Nicks for a jam session after school. My wardrobe consisted of three different pairs of jeans. She didn't appear to own any jeans, which blew my fashion-challenged young mind.

Eva had a fully loaded, powerful body with the exaggeratedly feminine curves of a cartoon character. Like me, she was almost fully grown by age thirteen.

Also like me, she was aware that her womanly shape was somehow wrong for the setting we were trapped in. At the mall, the new power we wielded over the older boys was intoxicating. But within the walls of the middle school world, where it mattered, stick thin was the only acceptable size and shape for girls at that time. Daily we confronted the fact that our normal-sized bodies felt unwieldy and were considered wrong. Unlike me, Eva never had an ounce of fat on her muscular body. But we both had failed to be petite, so we seemed to be failing, period.

Everything about her was *more.* She laughed louder, smiled bigger, told dirtier jokes, took up more space in the room, and knew exactly which buttons to push to throw kids and teachers alike off-balance. She was feared by those who didn't appreciate her resistance to conformity and revered by those of us who knew how to spot the real deal—an authentic rebel. She broke every girl code I knew. Like most of my friends, I was trying hard to fit in, but Eva appeared to be trying to stand out. Later I realized she was not trying at all.

We grew closer throughout middle school, and by the time we entered high school, I understood much more about Eva. Her homelife was completely different from mine. Her parents had divorced when she was very young, and she was raised by a single mother who might have had bipolar disorder and definitely drank too much. Frequently manic or drunk, her mom vacillated between showing animated exuberance and hiding behind a closed bedroom door. Her father, a mythical figure to me, was rarely mentioned. Eva's extended family members were successful local business owners who helped her mother financially. From my simple meat-loaf-on-Tuesdays homelife point of view, Eva's proud, loud Armenian household seemed to revolve around a lavish, sophisticated, and extravagant lifestyle that offered plenty of exotic food and celebratory drink to anyone old enough to raise a glass. At Eva's house, champagne flowed, crystal sparkled, candles burned, voices carried, and pots steamed. Life was alive with feeling, color, and possibility.

When we entered high school, some bullying older girls developed an aversion to her *attitude.*

"Hey, Crazy! Where ya goin'?" The senior girls taunted her mercilessly in the hallway, day after day. "Need some help hauling that ass around?"

Still, Eva strode down the school hallway unashamed. Her thick jet-black curls bounced audaciously, untamed, down her back. She held her chin up and often wore a wide grin, like she knew an inside joke. Eva walked the hallways like a CEO on her way to an important meeting, no matter what those girls said or did to her. I'd never witnessed my sister Monica being bullied in school, but I knew she was more like me than like Eva. Monica would have retreated inward, frozen up, longed to disappear. But Eva defiantly insisted on being *seen*, whether anyone approved or not.

We both loved to write. Throughout high school, we wrote poems and traded funny notes, dropped slips of folded notebook paper in each other's lockers to make the long, tedious days more tolerable.

> *Sherry—My Angel Child,*
> *So how in the hell was your day?*
> *Mine sucked big-time! I enjoyed your note. I got a real firm grip on your detailed description of yourself after an exhilarating, chlorinated round in the disgusting gym pool. Sick!*
> *Bell time.*
>
> *Love,*
> *Your Only Virgin Friend*

The normal rules seemed not to apply at Eva's house, a dream scenario for me—an insecure, socially uncomfortable teenager with an inexplicable, insatiable thirst for alcohol. We did shots of Jack Daniel's at the kitchen table. We drank Moët from the bottle in Eva's bedroom. We took a twelve pack of Bud Light from the fridge and drank it at the nearby park.

After I turned sixteen and both Monica and Jessie had moved out of the house, I ran from the empty quiet and spent as many weekend nights at Eva's as possible. Monica's departure from our home had been strained. Following a failed first semester at K-State, she moved into an apartment and got a job as an assistant in a legal office, but I knew she wasn't doing well at all. She came by the house and picked me up to go driving around sometimes, but I saw her less and worried about her more.

Jessie, on the other hand, went to K-State when she turned eighteen, joined a sorority, and seemed to sail along a path that she made look easy. I knew this meant trouble was ahead for me, as I still spent most of my time at home alone in my room, and nothing seemed easy. When I was out, though, whether with Eva or other friends, alcohol was nearly always involved. Those were the only moments when I stopped worrying about how to lose twenty pounds, how to not go mute when a boy spoke to me, how to climb behind the walls at school and disappear.

The drive to escape my daily anxieties left me confused by what felt like a need to lie to my parents in order to get my emotional needs met. I was drawn to Eva's house like a stray cat begging to be fed. Her mother was generous and kind to me without fail, never once implying that I was intruding or overstaying my welcome. But she wasn't well, a fact I witnessed frequently.

One night, I bolted upright out of a deep sleep on Eva's living room sofa, startled awake by crashing sounds in the kitchen.

"Eva!" her mother's shrill voice called urgently. "Eva!"

Pots and pans clanged, sizzling sounds and garlicky cooking smells wafted into the living room, cabinets opened and slammed shut.

"*Mom.*" Eva spoke in the stern, exasperated parental voice she often used with her mother. "It's *four a.m.,* Mom. We're *sleeping.* What are you *doing*? Go to bed, Mom."

Her mother allowed Eva to guide her back to bed. As I drifted back to sleep, I wondered what she'd been cooking.

In a household where both stability and sanity seemed to be in short supply, Eva herself was forced to generate some. At my house, emotional messiness hid behind polite restraint. But at Eva's, the crazy was visible. This was deeply comforting to me, because it mirrored the chaos I felt inside. My sober, humble Irish German parents from Oklahoma farming families didn't stand a chance against the seductive circus at Eva's house, where no emotion was suppressed, and no thought filtered, before being shouted across the velvety living room. The banging of a middle-of-the-night cooking show was reassuring to me, proof of the insanity I sensed existed just below the surface bullshit of daily life.

But I took for granted everything I had that Eva didn't—the ability to step away when the craziness wasn't fun at all and she just wanted to be a kid. I didn't see the dark side of Eva's life then, only the freedom from oppressive conformity. The awareness that my parents loved me lived in every cell of my body, but as a teenager that love was difficult to feel. I'm sure it was difficult for them to feel my love too, as I drifted further away. At Eva's house, I was accepted even when I was a total mess—which I felt like I was most of the time due to the emotional pain that I didn't know how to name—and that acceptance felt like love, too.

• • •

I took a deep breath and said the words out loud for the first time.

"I think I'm an alcoholic."

Eva and I were both about twenty years old, lounging on her mom's ginormous California king bed. The familiar fragrance of vanilla musk oil and the smoothness of her expensive sheets gave the room the comforting feel of a soft cocoon.

"No, you aren't." Eva was direct and decisive, traits I admired and adored. I longed for a smidgen of her clarity. Her response conveyed that my statement was ridiculous, weak, distasteful to her.

I wanted nothing more than to be strong like Eva.

"Yeah, I know," I responded quickly. "Of course I'm not. It's hard, but I just need to set some rules for myself. Only party on weekends."

Eva nodded, stretching her arms. I rolled over onto my back, relieved to get back to the cocoon.

• • •

Several years later, I was living in Parkville, Missouri, and Eva was living with a roommate in Lawrence, Kansas, about forty-five minutes away. Now in our midtwenties, we weren't a part of each other's daily lives, but we tried to stay in touch by phone, and we'd get together every few months.

For the third time in as many weeks, the air conditioner in my depressing, barely furnished apartment was broken. I packed a bag in a matter of minutes, tossing in my favorite sandals in case Eva and I decided to go out. The idea of drinking strong, frosty margaritas and talking for hours with Eva was the only thought that kept me going. I was miserable—dripping with sweat, choking down rage following my exasperating call with the apartment-complex management. The dismissive response from the front desk triggered every feeling of being powerless and voiceless that lived in the recesses of my trauma-riddled twentysomething mind. The oppressive humidity of the July afternoon and the helplessness I felt in my life bore down on me. I couldn't get out of the apartment fast enough.

Eva and I had made loose plans to get together that day. I had tried to confirm by phone but kept getting her answering machine. Because plans with Eva were always dependent upon many factors that could change at the last minute, I never showed up without finalizing plans. But on this day, I was going to insist for the first time ever—even if it wasn't the best time for her. I needed her. I'd never felt the acute need for anyone more than I felt the need for her that day. I left one last message on her machine before driving to her place: "I'm on my way."

By the time I reached the front door of her apartment, I was calmer. The whole drive there I'd gone over all the things I'd share with her: my recent breakup, the latest friend/family/work dramas, the nightmare of the air conditioner going out midsummer. I knocked on the door and imagined falling into her arms, crying.

When she swung the door open, I immediately saw that she was pissed to see me.

"What are you doing here?" Her voice was sharp, accusatory.

"I left messages . . ." I stumbled over my words, retreating in shock. "My air conditioner's out. I had to get away. I needed to see you. I'm sorry . . ."

"This isn't a good time, Sherry." She reprimanded me as if I were an annoying neighbor who'd rudely stopped by unannounced. I glimpsed her roommate in the background, looking tense, and surmised that they were having a disagreement. Whatever was happening was clearly more important than me.

"OK. I'm sorry."

She shut the door.

I stood on the hot porch in shock, staring at the wooden door for a moment before running to my Ford Escort, where I sat and cried in the parking lot for what felt like an hour. I had nowhere to go.

I'd rather be with Eva for an hour than anyone else all day. I had once told Monica that when she'd asked me why I tolerated waiting for Eva for hours and her frequently canceling our plans at the last minute. In the back of my mind, I had always wondered if she was more important to me than I was to her. Would she simply let go if I did? But back then, I thought you were supposed to hang on no matter what.

◆ ◆ ◆

We did hang on. Throughout our thirties, our folded notebook-paper notes from high school evolved into lengthy emails. By then, she was married and had a beautiful baby boy. I was focused on my career. And sadly, I'd been right that day on her mother's giant bed all those years ago. I was addicted to alcohol at thirty-eight, just as I had been at twenty, and at every age in between.

I'd entered rehab following a late-night phone call with my former roommate, Jennifer, who convinced me that I needed to get help immediately. I was just desperate and scared enough to listen. The unwavering support I received from the few friends, family members, and coworkers whom I told was humbling. Monica was at the top of that list of supporters.

But Eva seemed unimpressed in a way that I didn't understand. Addressing the issue with her was beyond me at the time, so I ignored it. But my experience in rehab ignited a profound shift in me. I was beginning to see that I had allowed the needs of others to overwhelm me from an early age. I had slipped into a pattern of denying that I had any needs of my own. After rehab, I began to see myself as the center of my own life rather than an accessory to the lives of others. I'd spent my entire life orbiting others as if they were the sun. This was especially true of how I saw myself with Eva. Even though I wasn't sure how to do it yet, I was ready to be my own sun.

I was excited to share with Eva everything I was learning about myself, as well as the details of my new relationship. Back and forth we emailed: her with a toddler in Wichita and me three hours northeast in Kansas City. While her feelings about my stint in rehab remained murky to me, her feelings about Andy, the man I'd met there but whom she never met, came through loud and clear.

Of course, she was right about him. The fact that Andy was a bad idea was never in question—any fool could see that the relationship with was ill advised. He was newly divorced, and we were both fresh out of rehab. I knew even then that it was likely to implode and be a mess. But it was *my* mess.

I knew expecting my friend to be supportive of me in a relationship she didn't understand was a lot to ask, but I was still asking. I saw then, and see even more clearly now, that her concern was legitimate and came from a good place, but at the time all I could feel was her judgment and a sense of being controlled. Unfortunately, I was awakening to one unhealthy dynamic while entering another one. But I had allowed the opinions and judgments of others to rule me my whole life, and *that* was suddenly intolerable to me.

What does she want me to do, ask her permission to date someone?

I tried to address my concern in an email to Eva, practicing my newly acquired skill of naming my needs. I acknowledged her right to be concerned and kindly requested the space and patience to figure things out in my own time, in my own way. She didn't respond, but I felt good about expressing myself and thought that we had an understanding. I was wrong.

Three weeks later we spoke on the phone.

"I had a dream about you last night," she said.

"Yeah?" We frequently shared our vivid dreams, mining for nuggets of hidden wisdom, guidance from one or the other's subconscious.

"But I'm not sure if I should tell you about it."

"What do you mean?" Her tiptoeing had me on guard.

"Well . . . I dreamed you and I went out to dinner. You wore a pair of khaki pants that weren't flattering on you." She paused. "In the dream, I wasn't sure if I should tell you or not."

Silence.

I understood immediately that Andy was the khaki pants. I understood that Eva wasn't planning to respect my request.

Rage flared—hot, red, blinding. Further humiliation added fuel to the fire in my veins. I knew her comment wasn't about pants, but my mind flashed back to our last meal together when I had, in fact, worn ill-fitting khaki pants. In my heart I was back on skates again and she was pointing to my hair and laughing. Eva had always dressed better, looked better. I counted on her to love me despite my lack of judgment.

My body burned but my voice was pure ice.

"Frankly, *you* are not invited into *my* decisions about what *I* choose to wear."

She began to cry, a response that was not unusual for her. Eva had always been able to access her emotions, and she expressed them outwardly, freely. But when we were younger, and even still, my feelings tended to go deeper into hiding the bigger they grew. True to form, she wailed while I did my imitation of an ice sculpture.

"I've been . . . trying . . . to . . ." She sobbed. The last three words were shouted in my ear, sputtered out between gasps for air. Three words that rang in my head for days, weeks, years: *"Let . . . you . . . go."*

I emailed Eva later that night. I recognized that my attempt to stand up to her for the first time had been unintentionally harsh, possibly even cruel. We'd never had a fight like this, but everything was new to me post rehab. I was eager to learn how to fight and make up instead of falling back into my old pattern of swallowing everything for the sake of avoiding conflict.

When she didn't respond, I sent another message, asking if we could please talk. But as the days passed and my emails went unanswered, I realized that she'd meant what she'd said. She was letting me go. This fight, like the one I'd had with my ex-husband Dominic seven years earlier, the night before he left and never came back, hadn't just been a fight. It had been an ending.

The grief was electric—a bolt of sharp pain followed by a persistent, terrifying buzz throughout my entire body that lasted for weeks. But even though losing Eva seemed unthinkable, my grief was tempered by an odd sense of relief, and as the grief subsided, the relief grew bigger. I eventually saw that she'd done the right thing, maybe the only thing that could have been done at the time. The path of self-discovery that I'd embarked upon after rehab changed the way I showed up in relationships entirely. Loss was part of that path. I lost Eva. And more loss was ahead for me before I would finally turn things around for good.

• • •

Twelve years have passed since that phone call, which was the last time I spoke to Eva. She is raising two beautiful children with her devoted husband. By all accounts, she's living out her dreams just as I am.

Our final conversation took place exactly twenty-seven years to the day after we met at Katherine Jenkins's skating party. A master of words, a lover of stories, a seeker of signs from the universe, Eva would appreciate the poetic symmetry.

The poems we wrote in high school still live in the beat-up light-blue Mead pocket folder where I first lovingly tucked them when I was a teenager, along with other written treasures I'd save in a house fire. When I study her feminine, circular, animated handwriting now, I remember how each note, card, poem, and email from Eva once made me feel so important—seen and known and loved.

Time has done its healing trick, and with each passing year I've gained clarity about why the friendship ended. I don't think about us rekindling our friendship as I once did. I'm at peace with how things stand between us, as I feel certain she is, and I feel proud of us both for happily living our separate lives, remembering the gift that we once were to each other. We could reconnect now if we chose to, but neither of us has done so, which seems perfectly fine, too.

I no longer believe that we're supposed to hang on no matter what. In fact, many of the blessings in my life have come from my willingness to let go. Of course, it's wonderful when relationships can keep growing, and that's worth fighting for. But when they can't, it's entirely possible to heal separately and move forward. Sometimes we must let go of something we think we can't live without in order to find what we truly need.

I'm proud of Eva for having the strength to let me go when she did. The truth is that even though she said the words, I let her go back then, too. After the two emails that I sent immediately following our final phone call, I never tried again. I never called or sent a card. I never apologized or tried to fix things. I didn't play my old role of making things better no matter what the cost to me. All these years later, I see the ways that letting each other go was good for us both. I don't long for the friendship anymore, though sometimes I miss that younger version of myself who loved with total abandon and complete certainty. Maybe I don't miss Eva now, but I do miss *loving* her.

◆ ◆ ◆

After my plane lands, I navigate LAX like a pro, take an Uber to my Airbnb, and tuck myself into the unfamiliar but cozy bed. I open my laptop to peek at my messages, expecting Monica to check in on me. Monica, having survived the hellish early adulthood years of a person designed for a better sort of world, eventually found her way. A creative genius, she quilts, decorates, makes jam and homemade jewelry, and operates an online used-clothing store. She also owns a successful pet-sitting business that requires her to drive around the city for hours each day, which she still loves to do. And, a bonus for me, she's one of the funniest human beings on the planet. When I told someone my dog was adopted, she quickly added, "He's not her biological dog."

After the accidental codependence in our teen years, Monica and I are now close in a healthy way. In our fifties, after twenty-five years of living hours apart, we finally live near each other. We get together often and exchange emails daily. She has no idea about my encounter with the boots earlier today, so I'm amazed when I open her message:

> I just came across some old letters I wrote to you from the dorm when I was eighteen. It was mostly incredibly sad remembering those days, but I did crack myself up with a joke I had written, which is one thing I want to remember about myself back then. "Well, I feel like studying now, so I'm going to lie down until the feeling goes away." I am so not that very lost girl anymore. Good stuff.

I send a quick reply:

> I'm in bed. All went well.
> We really made it, didn't we?

I close my laptop, turn off the light, and think about how far we've all come.

PERSONAL REFLECTION QUESTIONS

1. If you've experienced the abrupt ending of a long-term friendship, how did you handle it? If a lot of time has passed, do you see things differently now?
2. What are your beliefs about the importance of remaining connected with friends from your past?
3. In what situations is it better to end a friendship rather than try to repair it?
4. When a friend is in a relationship with a partner whom you disapprove of, what do you believe is the right thing to do?
5. How do you and your closest friends navigate your differences? How do you overcome disagreements?

CHAPTER SIX

Beasts

Jack Trimpey smiles back at me on my computer screen. I feel as if I've known him for years after reading his book so many times, but he's meeting me for the first time today via video chat. I saved up my money in order to purchase a package of individual sessions with him. He looks like his author photo on the inside cover of *Rational Recovery*, only a bit older, scruffier. His eyes are warm and kind. His intelligence intimidates me. He doesn't mince words or waste time on small talk, which is refreshing.

The details of my addiction story aren't relevant in this approach, so he doesn't ask for them. I've sought his help because Rational Recovery is radically different from Alcoholics Anonymous, which hasn't been a fit for me. My failure to identify the voice of my addiction in a movie theater ten years ago following six weeks of sobriety caused me to give up on Rational Recovery. I'd resigned myself to accepting the message I heard everywhere: AA is the only way. But after many more years of failing to connect with the principles of AA, and of not feeling anything close to the bliss I experienced with Rational Recovery in my twenties, I wanted to try again.

Minutes into our first call, Mr. Trimpey dives into the topic of dual animal/human nature.

"Let me ask you." His tone is conversational, unhurried. "Are you your body?"

"No." I know this one! It's good to be older, wiser. I know that I'm a soul in a body. Unlike in my twenties and most of my thirties, I now know and like the soul that lives in this body. All the work I've done in therapy, the self-help books I've read, the maturing I've done in the last decade have prepared me. I'm ready for this now in an entirely new way.

"That's right." His smile is genuine. "You need your body, but you are not your body."

I take careful notes, trying to capture each word:

I am not my body, but I need my body.

My body is an innocent animal that I am responsible for, like a horse.

Animals are not civilized. Animals only know now.

My body wants a drink. I am not my body.

I am a human being, uniquely capable of mastery over my animal nature.

This is not like meeting with a therapist. He talks more than he listens because he's teaching, not counseling. He doesn't ask about my feelings, my stories, or the ins and outs of my struggle. That isn't a part of this process.

I relish hearing the concepts from the book directly from its author, and as he speaks, I write:

It *is the Addictive Voice.*

It *comes from the midbrain, the reptilian part of the brain.*

It *is easy to recognize—any thinking that supports drinking comes from It.*

It *is powerless.*

It *plays with my language center, pretends to be me by using the pronoun I.*

Mr. Trimpey refers to *It* by the name Beast[3] because he says *It* is similar in nature to a jungle animal with survival instincts but no human consciousness. He explains calmly, clearly: "*It* shuts the lights out and you go into jungle time, animal time. *It* appears as a light that outshines everything, obscures survival, promises paradise. Following the false light obliterates life, leads to an intrusive, nightmare-like experience. Behind the bright light is a dark hole, a living death."

I nod. I know that bright light, the dark hole, the living death, the endless night of jungle time. I hold

---

3. The term *Beast* is part of the Rational Recovery method developed by Jack Trimpey and can be further explored in his book *Rational Recovery: The New Cure for Substance Addiction* (New York: Pocket Books, 1996) or at rational.org.

eye contact with my teacher, but my mind drifts. The talk of beasts has tripped a wire in my brain. For a moment, I'm back in an old life, a different jungle.

• • •

I straddled the enormous man on the living room floor of my apartment and pinned his hands down to the floor easily, because he let me.

"You will *never . . .* threaten . . . me . . . again." My words were measured as I stared into his dark blue eyes.

For a split second, he was frozen with shock, then he gave a tiny smirk—or was that small smile a hint of respect?

I ignored his reaction. He always ignored mine. "Do you *understand*?"

He didn't, but I did. At least I was *beginning* to understand the rules of jungle behavior. My dramatic table-turning moment didn't bring about the end of our relationship. This brief glimpse of the strength I had inside sparked my hope, but it would be months before I was able to get out of the relationship for good.

I had been twenty-four when I met twenty-eight-year-old Richard, an ambitious graduate student with dreams of becoming a lawyer. Mutual friends had introduced us, and we quickly fell in love. Two months later, Richard was a law school dropout with no home, no car, and no job. He was now also my fiancé. When he'd told me that he had borderline personality disorder, I wasn't scared, because I had a family member with that same diagnosis. My compassion for those struggling with mental illness had been further deepened by my own battles with depression. When he told me about his past psychotic episodes, I wasn't alarmed, and I remained unconcerned until the day my ponytail became a handle for him to use to yank my head backward. That's when my education really began.

Mental illness and abusive behavior are, of course, entirely separate situations. But during my time with Richard, I learned about the horrors a partner can experience when the two are combined. I learned that physical violence is not necessary for one person to effectively terrorize another. I learned the skill of acting—how to act as if the smell of his skin didn't repulse me, how to act as if I were fine so that no one would try to intervene and unintentionally make things worse. How to act warm when my heart was frozen.

"Are you OK?" I'd ask whenever he looked sullen, just as he'd trained me to do over a period of months by holding me hostage with his rage for hours if he felt I'd slighted him. Without overtly naming it or understanding it consciously, we both lived under the unspoken agreement that I was responsible for managing his feelings. If he felt or did anything bad, I was to blame. My inability to identify the problem with this way of thinking was my own sickness.

I paid a high price if I failed to keep him happy—hours of his angry sulking, blaming attacks, threats, or intimidation. I was emotionally well enough to know that this behavior was wrong and that I didn't deserve it. I knew I needed to get out of the relationship. But by the time I realized it, I was terrified. I believed if I left him, he'd kill me or himself.

So instead of leaving abruptly, I decided to exit slowly. I knew leaving this way was manipulative and extremely risky, but I couldn't see another way to get out safely. I decided to abandon my tacit agreement that I was responsible for his feelings, but not to *act* like I had. This small inner rebellion allowed me to see more clearly what was happening between us instead of feeling guilty.

When attending to his emotional needs, I began to modulate the level of concern in my voice to cover the fact that I no longer gave an actual shit. That is, I acted as though I cared more than I did, although not as much as I had. My plan for ending things was to reveal my emotional detachment ever so slowly. I banked on the fact that he'd eventually feel unsatisfied for reasons he couldn't quite put his finger on, and then he'd get bored and move on.

At the beginning of my extrication plan, I aimed for "Stepford wife" level of distance, then graduated to "nice coworker," before backing my way out to "friendly stranger." Along the way I played the game he'd trained me to play by attending to his moods with my words, even as I was dialing back my demonstrations of genuine interest in barely detectable increments. Withholding attention completely wasn't an option for me. Not if I wanted to stay safe. If I didn't inquire about his feelings, trouble arrived, as it did one Sunday afternoon in the living room of my apartment.

"You have *no idea* what I go through when you ignore me," he snarled in my left ear, holding my head back by my hair and exposing my neck. "You have *no idea* what I am capable of doing to you."

He was wrong about the second part.

I believed that my only way out was to outsmart him, so I settled in and played the long game. I realized that the only way to save myself was to never feel guilty or responsible for him, and that once I did this, he'd have nothing to feed on. But my retreat couldn't be sudden. There are certain beasts a person can't run from and expect to live. You can only back away slowly, praying they lose interest and go hunting elsewhere.

By remaining committed to my decision to never again feel guilty for his feelings or behaviors, my plan eventually worked. One day, following an intense explosion, he left. The hardest part was making myself not soothe him afterward like I used to do after a fight. But I didn't, and for some reason this time, he moved on.

By the grace of God, even though we were briefly engaged, Richard and I had never married. Still, although it had taken only two months for me to get locked in, and despite my one sweet moment of revolt, it took a full year for me to get out.

• • •

I emerge from these vivid memories and refocus on my call with Jack Trimpey. He's speaking now about time. He explains how *It loves* the "one day at a time" concept because of the opening provided—there's a possibility of drinking. Not *today* but maybe *tomorrow*. And if maybe *tomorrow*, then why not *now*? And guess what? It IS *now*!

My Beast has no concept of time. In the jungle, the time is always *now*. *Sometime in the future* is the same as *now*, a conflation of time that keeps *It* always awake, excited, and planning. The result for me is a constant battle in my brain. Rational Recovery uses an approach that's the opposite of "one day at a time." It asks me to commit to the *never now* plan. I write:

My Beast only understands the concept of now.
My Beast wants to drink now, always.
I never drink now.
I never now drink.

Too bad for you, beastie.

The simplicity of the approach is terrifying, the accountability daunting. But I trust it. I remember how it felt to be free all those years ago, back when I was in my twenties and experienced those six weeks of blissful relief from the battle. I am willing to do anything to get that feeling back.

Rational Recovery is all about *now*, so there will be no putting off my decision. Jack and I both know that when the Big Plan is proposed, when I declare my intentions for the future use of alcohol, *It* will be desperate to convince me to stall and take more time to study and reconsider.[4] My Beast will warn me not to act too quickly. *Let's decide this tomorrow—and hey, that way we can drink tonight!*

The Big Plan question is coming. I am ready.

"So, Sherry, what is your plan for the future use of alcohol?" Jack Trimpey asks.

"I will never drink again." I say the words and listen for the chatter inside my head. I feel the rush of resistance as my Beast, my reptilian brain—

---

4. Trimpey, *Rational Recovery: The New Cure for Substance Addiction*, 131.

convinced that I will die without alcohol—squirms and screams like a trapped animal. But the difference in this now, unlike the other nows that have come before, is that I am aware of *It* and I am watching *It*. That means that I am not *It*. I am me. The part of me that wants to be sober and free is the real part, the divine part, the watcher, the soul in the body. She is well worth saving.

"Your Beast is paying close attention. What does *It* say about your big plan?" he asks.

I speak firmly, saying out loud the words *It* whispers to me: *"Yeah, right, sure, whatever. You know you'll drink again. How soon is this call over?"*

Jack and I smile at each other as *It* whimpers in the light, exposed and powerless.

I pounce. In my mind, this time I flip the Beast onto *Its* back, straddle *It*, and stare *It* down. I recognize the false bravado, the smoke and mirrors, the brutish show of faux strength designed to cover powerlessness. The beastly persona is familiar to me, like the men from my past who relied on intimidation and force when they felt insecure, out of control, powerless. I gave them power by believing they were stronger than me.

I am so *done* with beasts.

"I. Will. Never. Drink. Again."

Looking back now, I see that on the day of that call I had only a rudimentary understanding of Rational Recovery. The deeper concepts took time for me to fully grasp and appreciate. The beauty in the method is a clear delineation between two worlds. The first is the world that we inhabit when we operate from the primitive part of our brain and live like beasts (as active addicts do) in the jungle, seeking satisfaction through the body. The second is the world we inhabit when we operate from our prefrontal cortex (where our higher functions exist) and enjoy the uniquely human world of awareness and spiritual connection.

Once you understand the difference, there's no competition. One is the life of a dog, and the other is the life of a supreme being with limitless potential and love. I reentered the human world and have no interest in ever living like a dog again. I needed to feel that initial surge of empowerment that day, to imagine myself standing up to the beasts I'd spent my life fearing—the abusers, the bullies, anyone I allowed to control or belittle me. Later, I came to understand that my Beast is, in fact, a part of me and always will be—not a part to be feared or hated, just a part of my brain that I'm responsible for managing.

Saying that you'll never use again is the easy part. Every addict knows that. Those who eventually stop for good have made the commitment hundreds of times. The hardest part of stopping is learning how to live inside your own head without using an escape hatch when things get ugly in there. Because of this, I believe that addressing trauma and shame is a key component for an addict trying to break free. That's only my opinion, though, and it isn't part of the Rational Recovery approach. It doesn't matter, though, how you stop; what matters is *that* you stop. After that, the real work of changing the thoughts and feelings that drove the behavior in the first place can begin.

Twelve-step programs are designed to help addicts develop new thinking patterns and reduce shame. The framework is simple but requires commitment, study, and practice. Rational Recovery also requires commitment, study, and practice. The theoretical bases for the two methods are in direct opposition, and using them both at the same time won't work. Each has strengths and flaws, of course, but each method offers a way for addicts to change the way we understand ourselves and the world. They are certainly not the only two ways, but both do offer a path back to life following addiction.

Over my many years of trying to understand and free myself from alcohol addiction, I released loads of shame—primarily through therapy, coaching, and reading about others like me—and replaced my rigid, perfectionistic thinking with curiosity and self-compassion. These days, I focus on embracing the messiness and mystery of being human. My favorite part of me is my backstory—all the mess behind me that proves how fallible, deeply flawed, and incredibly resilient I am. Somewhere along this journey, I fell in love with my human consciousness, with the wild ride of being a soul in a human body. I accepted the truth that allowing the most primitive part of my brain to run the show came at the cost of losing everything good about being alive.

Through the work of caring for myself, of learning how to assert myself and set boundaries, my desire to escape faded away. Now I experience a measure of peace even in the hardest moments, because I know those moments are natural. My pain is authentic now—pure, precise, human, temporary—and not the murky, constant low-level depression that resulted from my escape attempts. I desire *life* now. The freedom from addiction and the joy I experience daily from knowing I never have to return are beyond my ability to describe.

Thank you, thank you, thank you, God.

PERSONAL REFLECTION QUESTIONS

1. Have you ever been in a relationship you knew you needed to leave but didn't know how? How did it end? What did you learn about yourself from the experience?
2. If you're currently in a relationship that you believe you need to leave but don't know how, please tell someone you trust and seek professional help if needed.
3. What is the difference between feeling powerful and feeling empowered?
4. Share about a time you've achieved a goal you previously believed you couldn't.
5. Write down three empowering thoughts to remember the next time you are facing a situation that challenges you to be courageous.
6. What are some reasons you know that you're resilient?
7. What hard situations from your past do you appreciate now as part of your story?

CHAPTER SEVEN

Tantrum

Over a decade ago, I became a marriage and family therapist. Believe me, I understood the irony when I entered the Friends University graduate program in 2007. How could a divorced, childless, obese woman with years of codependency and alcohol addiction behind her become a marriage and family therapist? The question worried me. Still, I knew I'd be a good therapist *because* of all the past messes in my life, not despite them. And, indeed, by the time I was working with clients, though I still had a lot of growing to do, I was securely on the path to emotional maturity. I was also well on my way to establishing myself as a professional who helped people seeking to improve their lives.

After I completed a counseling internship at The United Methodist Church of the Resurrection in Leawood, Kansas, I was offered a staff position and served as director of counseling ministries. During my next seven years on the church staff, I also owned a private psychotherapy practice where I saw clients during evenings and weekends. My life became the kind of life I had always dreamed of having—one full of kind people, fulfilling work, and a sense of purpose. But my codependent traits snuck in, and I slipped into workaholism. Work became the partner whose endless needs I felt responsible for meeting while neglecting my own. I loved my job at the church and I also loved my psychotherapy private practice, but I did both at full speed for years and began to feel worn down.

Still, I was healthier in many ways. I'd done a tremendous amount of work on myself, so I recognized in 2015 that I was filling that old, familiar void with too much work and, as always, with food. I took a leap of faith and decided to devote myself to building my private practice full-time, leaving the church position. My bold move paid off and the practice filled immediately. It was up to me to keep my work hours reasonable, which I did. At this point, I'd kicked workaholism, alcohol, toxic relationships, and, for the most part, self-rejection. Food was the last addiction that needed to go.

If you're not thin, you're physically ugly and unacceptable.

You'll be more worthy of respect, love, and joy when you're no longer overweight.

True happiness comes from seeing the right number on the scale.

I knew these were lies. After years of unlearning old, negative beliefs, I'd found my way to valuing myself even though I wasn't thin. But after three decades of battling with my weight, I still carried nearly one hundred extra pounds. I had reached the point where my longing for freedom had become greater than my desire to be comfortable by stuffing my feelings down. I see now that the life-changing moment that occurred wasn't random at all; it was invited. I had made the terrifying decision to trust myself and quit the "safe" job. I had acted on faith. Next, I became determined to finally free myself without knowing how, exactly, I could do so. And then, seemingly out of the blue, the answer arrived.

One October afternoon I was in my bedroom, drying my hair, when a familiar thought crossed my mind but struck me as important in a new way. I put the hair dryer down and sat motionless, listening.

If weight loss is simply a math problem, what's really stopping you?

The whispered question came from deep inside, with no trace of judgment or condemnation.

I became aware that God was present with me in the quiet room. I don't mean God as a white-haired old man or an apparition. No, the God I experienced that day wasn't outside of me at all. Rather, the God I felt was the origin of light, love, life, and me. A God as faceless and genderless as time was both with me and inside me.

I know it's supposed to be simple: consume fewer calories and burn more calories. But there's so much more. You just don't understand, came my silent, defiant answer.

I'd like to understand. What do I not understand?

Well . . . it's just . . . *not fair.*

Oh.

The gentleness of the response made room for something inside me to open up. Until that moment, I'd had no idea of the anger I carried. But there it was. Slowly over the moments that followed, I recognized how deeply that anger ran. I was enraged by what struck me as the unfairness of it all, and I mean *everything.*

I was angry over the fact that babies die, that human beings are born into hellish conditions they never escape, that the wrongly accused are imprisoned, that unspeakable acts of viciousness are depicted on the news for our entertainment, that kids are cruel to each other and leave lifetime scars, that no law guarantees justice or equality. I was angry that so many teenagers are depressed, anxious, addicted, and suicidal. I was mad that I did not seem to fit in anywhere and never had. Mad about all I had lost and that my heart was so broken. I was even mad that I could not find anyone to be mad at anymore. And I was *especially* mad that I was expected to face all this without a smoke or a drink or some good old-fashioned relationship drama. Couldn't I at least have the freaking doughnuts?

And then it hit me: For years, I'd been throwing a prolonged inner tantrum while God patiently waited for me to wear myself out. The world was not set up to my liking. Life was harder than I'd prefer, thank you. As this inner dialogue unfolded, I saw that I had a choice. I could continue crafting my strongly worded letter of complaint, or I could let us both off the hook—God for not making life easier and me for expecting things I had never been promised and resenting the fact that I never got them.

God and I sat together and considered my dilemma with compassionate curiosity. I was ready to listen. In a clear voice, which felt to me like God speaking to me and through me, God told me:

Being angry at reality is a child's game. You got stuck when you started turning to substances to soothe your pain, which kept you from getting this sooner. But you're getting it now and that is good. Yes, the world is a hard place, but you were specifically created to be a part of it, and your light is needed by others.

When you fight with yourself and me, when you try to escape the natural hardships of life, you create a false reality that is unnaturally painful and not at all what I intended for you. The natural pain that comes with being alive is not a punishment. Heartbreak is not an exception. These are part of the human experience. Once you stop longing for things to be different or trying to find ways around the parts that are hard, you become open to a different kind of pleasure and beauty.

As I listened to this message unfolding inside me, I didn't shake my fists, break down and cry, or fall to my knees—actions that I had previously thought accompanied moments of spiritual breakthrough. The encounter was remarkably undramatic. I just suddenly knew. I finally knew that the hardest things about my life had been caused by my attempts to avoid the hardest things about life. I knew that the things I had not been equipped to handle when I was young, I was equipped to handle now.

My internal war, which had started when I was a teenager, was over by the time my hair was dry. My battle with reality had only taken about four minutes to resolve.

Thirty years and four minutes.

• • •

Six months later, I'm standing on a stage holding a microphone. In front of me, three hundred women and men sit in the large room at my church, my place of employment for seven years. I've stood on similar stages over the years as I worked to overcome my natural shyness in order to teach.

Today, the participants sit in groups of eight at round tables, their notebooks opened, pens poised. To my right stands my former supervisor, Reverend Karen Lampe, who's leading this three-day seminar. She developed a program to train church volunteers to assist pastors in providing care to their congregations. Her Congregational Care Minister program is nationally recognized. Clergy, church staff, and volunteers travel from across the country to attend this yearly seminar. As a mental health professional, I have the job of teaching guidelines for appropriate physical and emotional boundaries for church caregivers as they work closely in their service to others.

Karen introduces me and I greet the audience. My smile is easy, my body calm. I feel lit from within. I'm exactly where I'm supposed to be right now, and I know it—a fantastic feeling. Since leaving my staff position at the church to operate my private practice full-time six months ago, I've lost fifty pounds. My entrance into the event room this morning created a buzz from colleagues and friends, who responded to my changed appearance with happy surprise.

"You look amazing!" I heard from several staff members and church volunteers whom I hadn't seen in months. "Oh, wow! Look at you!"

One of the Congregational Care Ministers at our church, a delightful woman named Jan who struggles with her own weight, lavished me with praise for my achievement when she saw me. There to assist with the hosting duties at the event, she'd saved me a seat at a table near the stage. I sat next to her as I awaited my cue. Just before it was time for me to walk onstage, she leaned in and whispered in my ear, "How did you do it?"

"I discovered a magic pill," I joked. I hadn't been prepared for her question but didn't intend to be sarcastic. I smiled. "No. I'm just eating better and working out a lot."

But when the sides of her mouth turned down slightly and she looked disappointed, I realized she hadn't been asking *what* I did to lose the weight, she was asking *how* I'd done it. This was a very different question deserving a much better answer.

For now, I push the exchange with Jan out of my head to focus on the job at hand. The audience is primed and eager to learn. Boundaries are my favorite topic, but I know that they're challenging and confusing for many, especially for helper types like me. I enjoy teaching about boundaries because my entire adult life has been centered around learning to understand and love them, and everything I've learned, I've discovered the hard way. I have plenty of examples to share about my own boundary failures and what I've learned from those experiences. Karen's message throughout the curriculum is *teamwork, teamwork, teamwork.* Yes, yes, yes.

Karen and I demonstrate teamwork throughout the ninety minutes that we cofacilitate. Our camaraderie is apparent, our repartee infused with genuine affection. I adore Karen. She saw potential in me years ago when I first joined the staff, and she helped me develop leadership skills and grow from a counseling intern to a director in a short period of time. She is a petite powerhouse, known for her ability to walk across the massive church campus in record time, her tiny feet moving so fast they appear to barely touch the ground. She's equally well known for her intensity and passion. She has the physical grace of a ballerina and the efficient energy of a power saw.

Last year I stood on this same stage next to Karen, who can't weigh more than one hundred pounds, at my all-time-high weight of nearly two hundred and fifty pounds. To speak in front of a large group at that weight required significant mental preparation. Over the years, I'd learned how to speak in front of crowds despite my fear that my appearance would be negatively judged. That decision to push through my discomfort and take a microphone was a game changer. I found the courage to do it only because the alternative—silencing myself, out of fear—had become intolerable to me. Working with Karen, who was devoted to the empowerment of women, strengthened my feminist spirit, and I vowed to never willingly participate in the way that our culture frequently leaves women feeling unseen, unheard, and undervalued as leaders.

In the years that I was a therapist on staff at this megachurch, I'd been shocked by how far we as a country still have *not* come in the area of gender equality. Woman after woman had entered my office with tales of intimidation and physical and emotional abuse at the hands of a boyfriend or husband. Many of these women expressed to me that they felt trapped in abysmal circumstances; many cared for their children while feeling terrified to leave their abusive situation due to financial dependence or fear of retaliation.

Even though I'd worked in a domestic violence shelter, I was still stunned by the pervasiveness of the problem. I'd naively believed that women with access to education and resources were empowered to make healthy choices. I saw the lack of women in leadership positions in our society and realized that as long as women like me sat quietly on the sidelines—because we're too shy, or too insecure about our appearance or our capabilities to stand up and speak—our voices would never be heard.

I couldn't complain about the repercussions of gender inequality while avoiding opportunities to lead. So I decided that I'd never let myself decline a chance to lead because of a lack of belief in myself. I would "get over myself" in order to honor the women who fought for me to have the freedoms I enjoy. I didn't know it then, but my commitment to this higher agenda saved me by teaching me that I have value that is separate from my appearance. For all of us, but especially for women, this is a massive hurdle to overcome.

On my way home from the presentation, I unwrap and take a bite of the jumbo chocolate-chip cookie left over from my lunch. Six months into my healthy-eating plan, I know how to enjoy this exception without fear or guilt. I chew slowly and savor every delicious bite. I relish my earlier accomplishment of teaching onstage and replay the supportive comments about my weight loss. I wasn't losing weight to get attention or approval from others, but the validation of my reality is sweet. I *feel* like a different person inside, and it's wonderful to know that others can see that something is different, too.

I feel joy—my chest expands and my stomach flutters pleasantly. I now allow my feelings to flow through me. I invite them to hang around for as long as they need to, and I let them stay without judgment, without ignoring or stuffing them down. Before I made the commitment to feel all my feelings completely—no matter what—I would've wolfed down the oversized cookie immediately while on my way to buy more cookies to "celebrate" my public-speaking victory. Of course, my real goal then wasn't celebration but avoidance of my own thoughts and feelings. Even the positive ones could overwhelm me before I developed the ability to process intense emotions with self-compassion.

I ponder Jan's question from earlier about how I lost the weight and feel bad that I brushed her off, as if the answer were simple. I consider calling her to offer a more thoughtful answer. But what would I tell her? How *did* I do it?

The answer, ultimately, *is* very simple, I realize, but it's not "eat better and exercise." Those are commitments to myself that I've been able to keep *because* of the simple answer. The simple answer is self-love.

On that day that God and I conversed as my hair dried, I had discovered my hidden anger—and that had been a turning point. Days later, I'd started a healthy-eating plan, but this time was different from my past attempts. This time I approached my relationship with food as though I were a kindhearted investigator instead of an angry prison warden.

Curiosity and acceptance were my guides, emotional growth my agenda. Weight loss would be just one outcome of these deeper goals, and not at all the most important one.

After I'd acknowledged my inner battle with reality that day with God, I had begun to wonder: What other hidden beliefs are driving me? What other feelings lurk under the surface?

I had stopped fighting with God and gotten curious about myself.

That's how, I think as I finish the cookie. *Acceptance and curiosity. When you put them together, they feel like love.*

PERSONAL REFLECTION QUESTIONS

1. Have you ever experienced a spiritual encounter or sudden moment of clarity?
2. Has a commitment to a higher purpose ever changed your life?
3. If asked how you accomplished the hardest thing you've ever done in your life, what would you say?
4. What are some "failures" in your life that you later realized were important parts of your learning process?

CHAPTER EIGHT

Untethered

A disturbing flash of heat rises from my gut. Envy. Pure, sharp, intense. I'm with my friend Elaina, a woman nearly twenty years older than me. In her midsixties, she wears her thick, luscious hair—tons of it—loose and wild. I collected another sickening handful of my own hair from the shower drain this morning, placing the strands in a plastic bag, along with the date written on an index card. I'm going bald at forty-eight, and it feels like a bit of my sanity is slipping away with each strand.

My doctor has assured me that the hair loss is likely being caused by the fact that I lost ninety pounds so fast. So *fast*? The last year and a half has felt like a decade of tracking calories and working out. Still, even though it hasn't felt quick, I've loved the process this time, relishing each little victory. But as I've come closer to reaching my goal, an unfamiliar anxiety has crept in. As my body morphs, the familiar protection that my layers of fat provided dissolve, leaving me feeling exposed. All the buried traumas related to my body image surface. I see my therapist. I work with my life coach. I search for new books to feed my mind with spiritual matters, and in my search, I come across and immediately order the book *The Untethered Soul* by Michael Singer. I'm doing all I know to do to help myself. Still, anxiety and grief about my hair loss consume me.

"It's normal to lose about a hundred hair strands in the shower," Dr. Lester reported while examining my scalp. She seemed not to notice the urgency in my voice. She didn't understand that the butterfly was emerging from her cocoon only to realize that spring had long since passed. I didn't know how to express the fact that part of me still believed, deep down, that I had to be physically attractive according to a very specific standard in order to be worthy. Even if I'd known how to express this, Dr. Lester's office didn't seem like the place to do it.

"Well, this isn't normal. This is totally freaking me out." This profound statement is what I came up with instead.

"I can give you a referral to a specialist, a dermatologist who specializes in hair loss," she offered, refusing to get on board with my panic.

I accepted her offer, went home, and continued to collect and mark the evidence of my hair loss.

Measuring the degree to which I was losing my mind was a more difficult task.

That evening, following my appointment, I looked up the dermatologist and discovered she specialized in transplanting hair—an expensive, painful, and, to me, entirely unacceptable solution. But since my generation believes we don't really need doctors now that sites like WebMD are around, I foolishly diagnosed myself with alopecia. Subsequent obsessive middle-of-the-night internet searches revealed additional devastating facts, including the fact there is no cure.

My research introduced me to a bleak underground world of hairless men and women who shared stories of heartbreak, lost self-esteem, and endless failed attempts to find a solution that never materialized. I didn't find a single story of miraculous regrowth. One YouTube video showed a thirty-something woman named Liz demonstrating how to properly wear a wig, and this touched me deeply.

Though I never added to the conversation, I felt overwhelmed with gratitude for the wig lady and my new bald online community. But this gratitude failed to make me less distraught. I cried for us all, night after night. Adding to my pain was the deep shame I felt at mourning something that seemed so silly, vain, and unimportant. I had no cancer. No illness. No good reason to feel this sad.

My daily thoughts about my hair loss gradually morphed into a quiet obsession. When I reached up and touched my head, I felt the hair of a person I didn't know, thin and short and barely there. Every time I did this, my equilibrium faltered, and I questioned every choice I'd made in my life. At two in the morning, several nights in a row, the terrifying thoughts spiraled. I shot up, short of breath, sweating.

I'll never find love again if I go bald.

I never had love in the first place.

I never knew how to love or be loved.

My life is winding down, all traces of youth fading, and I did everything wrong.

The dark thoughts stirred up memories, specific moments from my past playing in my mind like movies on a screen. In one of these movies I was in my midtwenties, hating the very same hair I now so desperately mourned losing.

• • •

"Is this the woman who's engaged to Dominic Martin?" The caller ID on my cordless phone, standard for the midnineties, read "Unknown Caller."

"Um, no. Who is this?" I used my thumb to shift down the volume button on the TV remote.

"My name's John. I'm an old friend of Dominic's. I heard he was engaged to someone named Fiona, and I got this number. Are you Fiona?"

"No. This is Sherry. Dominic is my boyfriend." My heart pounded. "Who is this again?"

"I must have the wrong number. Sorry." He hung up.

I sat, stunned. I had never heard of a friend named John, which was no surprise since Dominic's entire life was shrouded in mystery. In fact, in a year of dating I'd never met a single friend of his. Months ago, I had done a bit of lazy sleuthing, made a call or two based on tiny bits of information I had gathered. But I never discovered anything that would disprove his unlikely stories. I gave up easily, shoving my suspicions to the back of the denial drawer with all the other junk.

Engaged. Fiona.

My head rang. My phone rang again, showing "Unknown Caller."

"Hello?" I grabbed it, breathless.

"Oh my God." A woman this time, crying. "My name is Fiona. I'm engaged to Dominic. I found this number on his phone and had my friend call to see if . . . oh my God!" She sobbed uncontrollably.

The denial drawer flew open, spilling out the ugly proof of a thing I had known but not known.

Dominic's outrageous betrayal simultaneously made perfect sense and completely blindsided me.

It's difficult now to remember a time before internet search engines made it easy to get the goods on a person. It's equally difficult for me to picture a version of myself who could so easily believe a man who told me he had a college degree, a military background, a corporate sponsorship from Adidas to run marathons, and a nasty ex-wife who kept him from seeing his young daughter.

Dominic had also told me that he'd lost all his belongings, including any evidence of the aforementioned life, in an airline luggage debacle when he moved to Kansas City from Seattle several years before we met. The former me he told this to was twenty-seven, a bit reclusive, a bit depressed, a bit alcoholic, and more than a bit naive. She had never encountered someone who was an expert at selling an altered reality. Dominic's stories seemed plausible, if just barely, and exciting and worldly, neatly confirming my younger self's lack of sophistication. One or two of his stories even turned out to be true.

Red flags had been flapping hard since day one. He professed his love for me only a week after we met. It was late July at the time, and we were sitting close, watching TV at my apartment in Parkville, Missouri. We'd met at a bar, and it never occurred to me to expect him to ask me out to dinner or a movie.

My failures adding up, my traumas unattended, I had stopped expecting things for myself. Just hanging out at my place seemed to be as much as I deserved. I certainly wasn't expecting any kind of declaration.

"Whoa, are you kidding?" I pushed away from him. We were sitting on my cheap blue-and-white pin-striped sofa. Up to that point in the evening, I'd been primarily concerned with hiding the enormous safety pin that was holding up the zipper of my old shorts. I was not at all prepared for this.

"I love you. I know it's fast, but I just know. You're everything I've ever wanted."

Dominic was small and wiry, with black curly hair and dark brown eyes so alert he looked like he'd just overdosed on caffeine. He was alive with an energy that vibrated. Part Italian, part Hispanic, part Tigger, he kind of bounced when he walked. It was easy to believe he was a marathon runner, as he claimed. He looked like he could knock one out and go for a brisk jog afterward. That intensity was the primary source of my attraction to him. He had so much life in him, while I felt so little.

"This is *waaaay* too soon. You don't know me at all." I felt disappointed. He was clearly off his rocker.

"I know. Please don't freak out. I just want a chance to show you. But I do have to tell you something."

Eyes wide with apparent trepidation, he confessed that he'd lied about his age. He was thirty-four, not twenty-nine.

OK. Weird. But who cares?

Then came the bombshell: He had also lied about being divorced and was only separated.

I felt and did all the requisite things. Aghast and appalled, I asked him to leave, and after an hour of groveling, he did. If not for loneliness, Jim Beam, and my pesky low expectations, that might've been the end of Dominic and me.

But it wasn't. A year later, Dominic and I were still seeing each other. I loved his energy, his constant efforts to make me laugh. My physical attraction to him made me keep taking him back whenever I got mad at him, which usually happened when he'd cancel plans or disappear for long stretches. I was drinking heavily, though, so I was disappearing for long stretches in my own way.

Obviously, I realized as I spoke with Fiona on the phone, staying with him had been a terrible mistake. But I didn't feel angry for myself. Instead, I felt terrible for Fiona. Minutes into my first phone call with her, I believed I was done with Dominic for good and found myself calmly consoling her. My kindness threw her, and in our mutually vulnerable states, we bonded like war buddies. After spending hours on the phone over the next few days—sorting through

Dominic's intricate lies, comparing details from notes jotted on calendars, each of us desperately searching for solid ground—we decided to meet.

At six feet two, she was easy to spot in the Kansas City bar she'd suggested. I was prepared for her to be tall; I wasn't expecting a full-on Amazon woman. Everything about her was enormous in all the right places—expressive brown eyes, impossibly long black eyelashes, thick auburn hair, perfectly lined lips, gigantic white teeth, gravity-defying cleavage. Fiona looked like the woman I had always longed to be, the woman every man in the bar wanted. Her magnetic looks contained magic—and power. I was in awe of her, as were the men who stared at her, the men who didn't see me at all.

"You're really pretty," she said, looking down at me, her face showing disappointment and surprise.

I liked her immediately.

"You're stunning." I smiled, knowing this was not news to her.

"Dominic told me you were overweight and not attractive at all." She said this flatly, with no malice.

The words reopened my oldest wounds, but I chose to hold on to *pretty*. She shook her head, realizing long before I did how deftly Dominic had manipulated us both, consistently crafting whatever narrative served his interests best. Telling one woman that another woman is ugly, and therefore not a threat, is the oldest trick in the cheater's play-book, but I didn't know that then. I was meeting the woman my boyfriend had asked to marry him while we were still dating. I had no reason to trust his judgment about me. Still, I believed the cruel way he described me was the truth.

Fiona and I drank. We commiserated. We laughed. She was disarming, open, funny, bold, and warm. I'd told her over the phone that, as far as I was concerned, she could have Dominic—and I felt embarrassed now that I'd thought keeping him had been an option. I saw now exactly why he loved her. In my head, I let him go again. *Take him. I don't want him.* In the dim light of the bar, neither of us could figure out why we'd fallen for him.

"Want to have some fun with this?" Fiona asked after a few shots of tequila.

She shared her idea that we meet up with Dominic, act like we are into each other, and suggest a threesome. We knew this would freak him out, and he certainly deserved to be on the receiving end of our revenge. We also knew he would do whatever we asked because he would be terrified that he'd lost us both. Fiona called him and asked him to meet us at a different bar, and he agreed.

When we entered the second bar, where Dominic was waiting, a random drunk man looked our way and yelled across the crowded room, "I'm in love with that tall woman!" Fiona didn't even flinch.

Her acting skills turned out to be as impressive as Dominic's had been. She was quite convincing in her performance as she made eyes at me while the three of us sat at a small, sticky table with our bottles of beer, the drama of a smarmy daytime TV talk show crackling between us. I innocently enjoyed her attention, relished his discomfort, and wondered how the game would play out. We hadn't planned an ending for our vengeful plot, and it dawned on me as she placed her hand on my thigh that we'd never actually established that we didn't intend to follow through. I was way out of my league.

Dominic had a look of panic in his eyes when Fiona suggested heading back to her place for a drink, but neither he nor I was willing to back down from the dare, so we gathered our coats. I had no clue how I'd get out of this, but the option of walking away wasn't tolerable. It would only prove my fear that I was far too mundane to compete with a woman like Fiona. I just kept taking one more step forward, hoping one of them would back down.

An early fall frost had left the parking lot covered in black ice. Fiona, a self-professed klutz—a trait that only added to her charm—wiped out immediately. All six feet of her went down like an oak tree, and she landed hard on her ass. Dominic was at her side in an instant, helping her up tenderly with a genuine concern he'd never shown me. She leaned on him, limping as they moved slowly together toward his truck.

Until this moment, I wasn't aware that part of me hadn't accepted that Dominic and I were over. Deep down, I'd been hoping that he and I would fight it out and eventually, somehow, come out on the other side and laugh about all of this as he worked to earn back my trust. But in that frigid parking lot, I saw the truth. I saw a man I used to know. A man madly in love with a woman who wasn't me.

I pulled my coat tightly around me, ducked to my car, and drove home alone.

They got married three months later.

My rebound was fantastic. I started jogging, eating right, drinking less. I lost twenty pounds, changed my hair, and bought new clothes. I moved into a cool loft apartment with a recently divorced friend and started my life over. This time around, *I* was going to be Fiona. I transformed into a sexier, bolder version of my former self. I went to bars, and while no man ever yelled, "I'm in love with that average-height woman!" when I walked in, men noticed me now, and a few of them asked me out.

Less than a year after the threesome that wasn't, I was on a date with a guy named Mitchell, playing pool in a smoky bar, when I caught Dominic staring at me from a corner table, his eyes wide, jaw open. He was alone.

I hadn't seen Dominic or Fiona in months, but we had a few mutual acquaintances. It appeared that the rumor was true. He and Fiona were done.

In that moment, I learned that the sweet fantasy in which the previously rejected, ignored, and betrayed person morphs, in a Rocky-like montage, into the object of intense desire is, in fact, as deeply satisfying as every romantic movie ever promised. I leaned seductively over that pool table in my jean shorts and ignored him, hard.

After a while, I excused myself and stepped outside for some fresh air.

"You look incredible." Dominic appeared next to me on the sidewalk.

"You look divorced." I smirked, my head cocked to the side, hands resting on my newly chiseled waist. "Again."

He laughed, his eyes sparkling with the same sizzling energy I had once loved so much.

Shit.

Round two was different. He adored me, spent money on me, told me I was beautiful. When the hollow feeling crept in, I reminded myself that I had won. I'd become Fiona after all.

"What do you love about me?" I snuck in the insipid question one night when I knew I had his full attention. We were standing in the kitchen of my apartment as he reached for me.

"Oooo, so many things." Dominic's hands traveled slowly up and down my body.

"What exactly, though?"

A condescending chuckle, a pause, a hint of annoyance. "I love your eyes, and your smile, the way you walk . . ."

"Yes, but what do you love about *me*?" I pulled back and looked him in the eye. I longed for him to name something about me that he loved that wasn't physical.

"What do you mean? I love everything about you. But this"—he grabbed me lustily from behind and pulled me toward him—"*this* is the best part."

Peeking under an imaginary manhole cover for a split second, I pictured a massive underground warehouse where the correct answers to the test *What's Lovable About Me?* were stored, waiting to be accessed. I was asking someone who would never know the answers, and I was too scared to go exploring and find them on my own. I pushed the thought away and chose to agree with him; I was lovable because I was physically attractive to him. I let him take me into his arms and tried as hard as I could to let that be enough.

We got married three months later.

Six months after that, I sat in his beloved Seattle Seahawks armchair, waiting for him to return home, but he never did.

I moved out and we got divorced. This time we were done for good.

• • •

It's two a.m. I'm tossing and turning in my bed. Nearly twenty years have passed since I was that misguided young woman who sought validation from men because she didn't value herself. I'm grateful to be free from all the relationships from my past that weren't built on mutual trust and respect. I've filled my life with loving, reciprocal relationships. I know who I am. I love who I am. But in the past few weeks, I've lost my grasp of all of this in my exposed state, in this new body that doesn't feel like mine yet after losing so much weight and now losing my hair. I've temporarily forgotten everything I've spent the past decade learning.

The thoughts won't stop. I can't breathe. I don't want to be this shallow person who believes my hair is so important, my appearance so intricately linked to my lovability. I understand logically that such ideas are ridiculous, and I feel disgusted with myself for giving any power to the lie. I want to purge the faulty belief for good, but it feels as embedded in my being as if it were a part of my cells. I want to scrub my psyche of a lifetime of relentless messages that told me my worth is measured by my ability to look a certain way. I'm enraged, soul-crushingly sorrowful, a despairing and trapped animal. I howl. I scare my dog. I feel broken. I need to center myself. I need help. I need to hear the words that will bring me back to something I know but can't see clearly through my anxiety.

It's too late to call anyone tonight. The new book I ordered won't arrive until tomorrow, but I remember I can access a sample online, so I grab my e-reader and frantically open *The Untethered Soul*. The title of the first chapter is "The Voice Inside Your Head."

Yes! That line alone holds a familiar message— the truth I know deep down and am desperate to remember. I recognize immediately that this is the book that will get me down from the ledge. I consume the words fast, my heart rate slowing, my fear slipping away a bit with each paragraph until I come upon the sentence that restores me: *There is nothing more important to true growth than realizing that you are not the voice of the mind—you are the one who hears it.*

And I return to myself in that instant. I remember that this inner noise is just my mind creating scary thoughts because I'm grieving.

I remember that I'm a soul, in a body, with a mind. I remember what I've known for years now.

My *mind* makes up thoughts. My *soul* is the listener, the watcher. My soul was made by my Creator.

A deeply comforting awareness arrives, settling my body and quieting my mind.

I'm back. The temporary lapse is lifted. As I know how to do from years of practice, I replace the disturbing thoughts with thoughts rooted in a truth that overrides the buzzing of my anxious human mind. Grief and fear are part of being alive.

My soul is made of love and light.

Yes. Yes. Yes. I know this is true. I can feel it again. I let the truth flood in.

My hair doesn't matter, not really. My appearance has no connection to my worth or capacity to love or be loved. But it's also OK to feel sad that my body is changing with age.

I remember that my busy, fearful mind creates scary ideas not because I'm stupid but because I'm human. I have the power to observe them, to notice how my mind is trying to warn me or help me solve my problems. I can begin to gently replace these ideas with thoughts that hold much greater truths. And I can allow sadness to come, and even stay awhile.

I lean back on my pillow, take in air through my nose, and blow it out loudly into the night. My dog jumps back up onto the bed, gives my hand a tiny *welcome-back* lick, curls up next to me, and yawns.

What's lovable about me?

The old question from my days of seeking such answers from the men in my life resurfaces. Those men didn't know the answers because *I* didn't know the answers.

I let God answer this time. The manhole cover flies off, and answers stream out as free flowing as lava—overflowing, infinite, glorious.

You are precious and valuable—there has never been and will never be another you. You are beautiful because your heart is good, even if it's not always pure.

You are loved beyond measure, not because you earned it, but because I created you.

You are capable of limitless love—all you have to do is open yourself to it.

You are designed to bring light into the world.

You are forgiven.

I choose to believe it all.

PERSONAL REFLECTION QUESTIONS

1. If you've ever gone through an episode of anxiety or shame like the one described in this story, how did you get through it? Name two actions you can take if you experience one again.
2. In what ways, in the past, have you connected your worth to your physical characteristics? What do you choose to believe about that going forward?
3. What determines your worthiness as a human being?
4. Even after we fully embrace our own worthiness, we may face challenges— moments when we temporarily forget. In what ways will you help yourself remember?
5. What's lovable about you?

CHAPTER NINE

Now and Never

Valerie Bertinelli beams at me from my TV as she prepares a grapefruitini in her sun-filled California kitchen. Vodka never looked more innocent.

In my twenties, romantic movies provided me with a seemingly harmless escape, igniting and feeding my deepest fantasies. Invariably in these movies, an extraordinarily beautiful woman—depicted in the film as homely and invisible—randomly meets a kind, brilliant, gorgeous stranger, and they fall in love. She drinks wine, usually in a romantic dinner scene, but never overdrinks. Or, if she does, it's in a cute and funny way. Her hangover consists of an adorable headache she nurses for five minutes while looking stunning with her perfectly disheveled hair.

Sometime in my thirties, though, these movies started to piss me off. I lost my ability to indulge in this sort of fantasy around the time when Jennifer Lopez became the "everywoman" struggling to find love just like the rest of us. Once the relatable, good-hearted, overlooked maid or dog walker or wedding planner just happened to look like, well, *Jennifer Lopez*, I was done with the genre.

I was in my forties when I discovered HGTV and the Food Network, both of which promised a different sort of perfect life. But this one I could attain on my own, without waiting for an over-the-top romantic gesture from a handsome stranger who never showed up. (Presumably, he's out there looking for a kind, available dog walker or maid or wedding planner who just happens to look like Jennifer Lopez.)

Today, Valerie and her grapefruitini have me at hello.

It turns out that my Beast, the voice of my alcohol addiction, is cool with the switch from chick flicks to home-perfection fantasy shows. *It* can work just as easily with material presented by Jennifer or Valerie—any depiction of a beautiful life will do. On this afternoon in 2019, with my fiftieth year coming to a close, the grapefruitini has awakened *It*, and in a whisper as sweet as the spring flowers on Valerie's Los Angeles countertop, a gentle suggestion enters my mind.

It: *Ohhh, that looks refreshing!*

Me: Hi there. Yes, it does.

It: *Valerie enjoys a cocktail as part of a healthy life full of sunshine and flowers. I could do that now, too. So much time has passed. I'm so much stronger now—an entirely different person! All I need to do is decide to* never overdrink *again—the same way I decided to* never drink *again. I've proven to myself that I am powerful enough to always remain in charge, no matter what. So why not enjoy a drink, too? Remember how fun that was? That mess about being an "alcoholic" (is that even a thing, really?) is in the past. I could try drinking again, and then if it doesn't work out, I could just stop again.*

Me: *Hmm. You have an interesting theory. Let's play that whole story out, shall we?*

It: *Crap.*

Me: *Exactly. You are full of crap. Nice try, though! Nice to see you. In fact, it is amazing to* see *you.*

I play out the scene in my mind, mentally going through the process of deciding to drink. I imagine the first glorious sip of vodka and allow my brain to conjure the intense, unmatchable pleasure I'll feel as the burning liquid eases down my throat into my belly. I notice that even in the fantasy, I'm not able to experience the pleasure the way I used to because I cannot "unknow" what I know. I can never again *enjoy* the disconnection from myself the way I did in the past. Any pleasure associated with the experience of consuming alcohol is now inextricably intertwined with my awareness of the consequences. I can't pretend I don't know that one sip would bring on an overwhelming desire for another and another.

I don't fool myself into thinking otherwise. I have zero interest in consuming one fruity martini. I will *always* want the entire pitcher, followed by a second pitcher.

I know that I wouldn't remember much of anything beyond that first sip. The next day I'd be wondering what I did while I was gone—literally checked out of my own mind while my primitive brain did whatever felt good to my body. But the next-day sickness and regret wouldn't be the worst of it. The intolerable part would be reentering the hell I lived in for all those years while *It* taunted me daily. Empowered by the win, emboldened by the strong memory of a recent high, the voice of my addiction would chant in the background all day long: *More! More! More! Now! Now! NOW!* The incessant nagging one binge would ignite in my brain is a nightmare that no drink is worth to me.

It slumps away, defeated.

Me: *See ya!*

Valerie and her husband bring sugar-rimmed martini glasses to their lips, eyes gleaming with pleasure. I enjoy these fantasy shows, not because I think a perfect life exists the way they portray it on TV but because it's fun to watch pretty people create things.

I imagine the crew filming the scene, the unfinished cocktails tossed in the sink after the director yells "Cut!" The difference between Valerie and me is that a grapefruitini is no more important to her than the chicken she roasts or the cookies she bakes. But alcohol is extremely important to me, and it'll be important to me forever. There is a part of Valerie Bertinelli that can toss a half-full cocktail into the sink without an inner battle. There's no part of me like that, and there never will be. That's a reality that I accept. I'm at peace with the fact that a part of me would give up my whole beautiful life for a pitcher of martinis. The part of me that lives for alcohol will always be there watching, waiting for an opportunity.

But the good news is that another part of me, a far wiser, stronger part, is always there too, also watching, waiting for the opportunist to appear. I'm grown up enough now to know that Beasts don't show up in red capes, horns poking from their heads. They don't hide in dark alleyways that can simply be avoided. No. Beasts sneak in on lovely Tuesday afternoons and slither into the safety of a living room through a wholesome television program filled with family, flowers, and fruit. This type of Beast, however, loses all power when pulled out of the darkness and clearly identified. Light defeats *It* completely, every single time without fail.

As I always do after *It* crawls away in defeat, I say a prayer of gratitude. I thank God for allowing me to understand how my brain works, for granting me the ability to know how Beasts operate and for giving me the capacity to enjoy the freedom of choice in my thoughts and actions. I thank God for the deliciousness of life, available for me to savor.

I leave Valerie in my living room and enter my own sunny kitchen, where a grocery list sits next to the coffeepot. On the little blue notepad, under the words *almond milk*, I write *grapefruit*.

PERSONAL REFLECTION QUESTIONS

1. Make a list of things you've done in the past that you've decided you never need to do again.
2. If you wrote a book about your life so far, what would the title be?
3. If you were to write a book about the next five years of your life, what would its title be?
4. What makes life delicious to you?

PART II

---

*Further Insights and
Practical Application*

CHAPTER TEN

Thoughts on Recovery from Alcohol Addiction

Many people find success in AA and achieve long-term sobriety in the program. They overcome their inner rebellion and experience a beautiful surrender. It's truly a miracle. Some of the most amazing people I know went through this process and became shining examples of humility, kindness, and sober living. I have nothing against this approach and believe it's good for many people. But I don't believe it's the *only* way to achieve sobriety or humility.

My own story didn't play out that way. This fact created a dilemma for me when I became a mental health professional. How could I encourage clients to seek a solution that had never worked for me when a different solution, one that directly opposes the standard approach and is not supported within the mental health community, *had* worked for me? This is a question I wrestled with privately for ten years.

As a licensed therapist, I did what I was trained to do and referred clients presenting with addictive disorders to industry-approved programs where the twelve-step methods were the primary treatment modality. I managed my personal feelings about this by not specializing in alcohol-addiction recovery and by not sharing about my own recovery process with clients. If you read *Rational Recovery*, you'll better understand why this was a difficult position for me to be in. Reading the book may also generate other questions, so I'll attempt to offer a bit of clarification for those who would like to know more.

Are you saying alcoholism is not a disease?

No, I'm not saying that. Medical experts say alcoholism is a disease. There are many good reasons for this. Identifying alcoholism as a disease helps with legitimizing the problem, reducing shame and stigma, and funding research. I'm not a medical expert, and I have no desire to argue for or against the disease concept. I continue to read and learn. When used to describe alcohol addiction; words like *disease, illness*, and *disorder* make sense to me. Clearly, there's a serious mental disturbance in a human being who knowingly risks devastating losses in exchange for consuming a substance not needed by the body for survival.

Are you saying addicts can recover alone?

No. But I am saying there are a variety of ways to recover with help and support. I've worked with fantastic therapists and life coaches in my own process over the years, and I received guidance and training from Jack Trimpey directly. I've also been surrounded by friends and family members who've loved me through it all. Choosing an alternate path to recovery does *not* mean that you do it alone.

Are you saying my addicted loved one is choosing this behavior?

Yes and no. Yes, a person consumes alcohol only by first choosing to do so. And no, they aren't choosing the brain malfunctions that occur when they ingest alcohol regularly. Until there is an effective disruption in an addict's *thinking* pattern, their brain response to the addictive substance will override their best intentions. But every addict holds the responsibility for seeking help and for the consequences of their addictive behavior.

Do you teach Rational Recovery?

No. Jack Trimpey developed and teaches Rational Recovery. He remains wisely vigilant about maintaining the purity of the model. But he'd be the first to tell you that everything you need to get started—and to get finished with drinking for good—is in his book, which I highly recommend to those who are interested. As I hope I've made clear, it is my personal recommendation that those who utilize this approach also access other avenues for mental health support in order to address shame and trauma, if applicable, and to create meaningful connections with others.

Many therapists and coaches now embrace alternative approaches to recovery. However, Rational Recovery remains a hard sell in the mental health field. In his book, Mr. Trimpey directly challenges the standard accepted approaches to addiction treatment and the mental health industry's involvement. The fact that I, a mental health professional myself, became a champion for his approach is unexpected, to say the least.

While I don't teach Rational Recovery or currently work with clients in the earliest stages of alcohol-addiction recovery, I do love working with clients who've obtained long-term sobriety by any means. A unique understanding exists between people who've made it out of addiction. No matter how we achieved sobriety, we now share a commitment to living differently and an acute awareness of the precious, fragile nature of our own sanity.

My areas of specialty, both as a therapist and now as a coach, are the skills that former addicts know are the keys to remaining sober—living authentically, managing thoughts and emotions constructively, communicating assertively, setting healthy boundaries, and honoring commitments we make to ourselves and others. These are life and relationship skills that are important for every adult, but for those of us who've seen firsthand what happens when we abandon ourselves to addiction and lose touch with all that matters, they represent so much more. For us, living authentically, managing thoughts and emotions constructively, communicating assertively, setting healthy boundaries, and honoring commitments we make to ourselves and others are the skills and practices that keep us alive and make our lives worth living. If you're in this category, I'm proud to be in it with you.

CHAPTER ELEVEN

Thoughts on Recovery from Codependency

I began to seriously study the concept of codependency when I was in my late thirties. At the time that I entered graduate school, in 2007, to study marriage and family therapy, I was determined to solve the greatest puzzle in my own history: Why would an intelligent woman repeatedly enter—and remain in—toxic intimate relationships?

It was easy to dismiss my earliest boyfriend debacles as youthful mistakes, which they were to some extent. Each time one of these relationships ended, I determined that the guy was a jerk and I was an innocent victim with terrible luck. But at a certain point, there was no denying that I was the common denominator in a long series of disastrous couplings. No matter how different from one another my partners seemed on the outside, I eventually felt the exact same way when I was with them—locked into a painful relationship that I found impossible to improve and even more impossible to leave.

After graduate school, where I learned about healthy relationship dynamics from the experts, I became a certified sex addiction therapist. For several years I worked on issues related to sex addiction with both addicts themselves and, even more frequently, their partners. During this time, my work with partners of sex addicts taught me that the word *codependent* can be triggering, especially when a person feels unfairly labeled or blamed.

I found the word to be useful to me personally, but I understand that not everyone feels that way about the term. I'd never want a person to feel negatively labeled or unfairly blamed. The solution—self-love and healthy boundaries—is the same no matter what you call it. I want to clarify that my comments in this discussion are focused on adult-to-adult partner relationships. Parents can have codependent relationships with teens and young adult children, too, but there are additional factors beyond the parameters of this particular book to consider in sorting through those dynamics.

Over the years, I've seen so many amazing, successful, smart, loving people follow the same relationship pattern that I did. Some were in relationships with addicts at the time they sought help, but some weren't. All of them, however, had been in *at least one* close relationship with an addict, a person with a mental illness, or a very controlling person at some point in their past. In every case, I discovered that the client experienced a lack of self-love and their current and/or past partners had experienced significant self-worth struggles, too.

From my professional vantage point over the past decade, I've observed no single pattern of behavior to be more prevalent than codependency. There are *millions* of us. And no, we aren't all women. I've worked with many men who struggle with these same patterns. We're the well-meaning helpers of the world, the relationship nurturers, the empaths, the sensitive souls. We have a huge capacity for storing emotional pain and, sadly, are easily manipulated by those who, intentionally or not, exploit our empathy and our difficulty setting boundaries.

Codependency isn't a mental illness or a diagnosis; it's a learned way of relating to others in close relationships. One characteristic of codependent people is that we feel *overly responsible* for another person's feelings and behaviors. We tend to love others *at our own expense*, which means that we confuse love with feelings of fear, obligation, and guilt.

I believe that it's more accurate to say that a codependent person lacks self-love and, therefore, doesn't uphold healthy emotional boundaries in relationships. Living without self-love or healthy emotional boundaries has destructive and even dire consequences. For this reason, I firmly believe that our intentional cultivation of self-love—not to be confused with narcissism or selfishness, which are entirely different states and behaviors—is the highest responsibility we have to those we love. Without some measure of self-love, we cannot and will not uphold healthy boundaries.

Codependency showed up in my life in a way similar to what my clients describe in their own histories. Because I had been ill-equipped to understand, manage, or honor my own emotions, a sense of "lack" developed deep inside. And so I found myself drawn to relationships where there was a lot to *respond* to—people with big personalities, clear opinions and desires, and the outward appearance of confidence (which masked insecurity).

I am a natural listener, supporter, and problem solver—great qualities, but when combined with an underdeveloped sense of self, they made it easy for me to disappear in relationships, to "hide" in them. I began to gain my sense of worth and connection by playing a specific role in my closest relationships— listener, supporter, problem solver—rather than developing and asserting a separate identity within them. This became my pattern, and over time, my unaddressed emotions, unhealed wounds, and hidden shame about myself compounded.

I connected in life most easily with others who had similar issues—unaddressed emotions, unhealed wounds, and hidden shame. This is the *co* in *codependency*; there's a *mutual* dependency. Both people depend on the relationship to satisfy individual needs that a relationship cannot wholly meet: a need for a sense of worth, a strong personal identity, and a feeling of self-love. Over and over, I discovered in my life that relationships built on this unspoken arrangement fall apart, often spectacularly and painfully. Or sometimes, as I witnessed in the lives of my clients, such relationships go on for years despite a frustrating lack of authentic intimacy that baffles both partners. The relationship can even look great on the outside, which creates added confusion to the partners and their families when things fall apart. What was missing in every single case, both in my own and in the relationships of my clients, was the sense of *self-love* that each partner must develop on their own. A sense of individual worth and identity must exist outside of the union before each person has the capacity to offer *selfless love* inside of it.

We codependents are devoted friends and partners who strike this unspoken bargain: *Your needs are enough for both of us, so I won't have any. I'm fine so long as you're fine.* But we're not fine. We do have needs. We just don't know exactly what they are or how to honor them. We take care of others, but our own emotional worlds are often deserted wastelands of unattended grief, hidden resentments, and persistent loneliness, despite our being surrounded by people who love us.

We neglect ourselves by obsessing about how to "get" our loved ones to see, think, or behave differently so that they will finally be happy, and so that we, thereby, can finally be happy, too. We avoid that scary place inside ourselves. Who *wouldn't* avoid going in there when the self-judgment is relentless, the emotions overwhelming and terrifying? Because of this very reasonable fear, it's nearly impossible to convince a codependent person not yet in recovery that they will find satisfying connections only when they stop trying to control things that are *way* beyond their control—namely, other people's feelings and choices. In order to become healthy, addicts must see their own behavior as a serious problem and become willing to commit to the hard work of changing their default behavior settings. The same is true of us codependents.

I've created a list of codependency traits based on patterns I've observed from my own past and on the most common behaviors I've observed in my work with codependent clients. Any single item on the list is worth addressing. But for those who show a combination of these traits, the effect is compounded. There's absolutely no need to feel ashamed if you struggle with these traits. These are learned behaviors that can, with concerted effort, be unlearned and replaced by new behaviors. At any moment, you can decide to start on a new path, one little step at a time.

Codependents tend to

- feel overly responsible for the feelings and actions of those we love;
- struggle to set healthy emotional boundaries and often tolerate boundary-violating behavior;
- stay in close relationships with people we feel sorry for or want to help, even when the relationships become detrimental to our well-being;
- experience difficulty knowing or directly expressing what we need, want, and prefer *separate from* the needs, wants, and preferences of those we love;
- have difficulty allowing our most tender emotions to surface; may fear being viewed as "weak" or "needy";
- avoid assertive communication due to low self-worth, use passive, passive-aggressive, and aggressive styles;
- be inwardly perfectionistic and shame-based, judge ourselves with relentless

harshness while easily offering compassion and grace to others;
- remain in unbalanced relationships
in which our loving actions are not
reciprocated.

The codependency recovery process *doesn't* start
with leaving your current relationship, although you
may decide that you need some temporary distance
to work on yourself. Whether you leave your current
relationship or not, the pattern will repeat until you
address the underlying problem. Recovery *does* start
with the decision to make your relationship with
yourself the most important one in your life. This
decision takes place entirely separate from any other
relationship you happen to be in now. If you think
this is selfish, that's a belief you'll want to challenge
right away, because holding on to it will keep you
stuck in this pattern. When your relationship with
yourself is truly loving and respectful, every single
relationship in your life will benefit exponentially.
Those who love you desperately need you to show up
fully as *you,* and that isn't possible if you're focused
on others to your own detriment.

Building your relationship with yourself starts
by checking in with your thoughts and feelings—
go inside and look around. Clean out the old junk
and start decorating to your own taste. Make it your

number one goal to create an inner world that you don't need to escape, and allow this process to take time. Fire yourself from the job of managing what others think and feel—another goal that will require time and practice. Let yourself off the hook for trying to get the people you love to be at peace with themselves or to behave more responsibly. You want them to develop self-love, but you may not have developed it yourself yet. You can't love someone into loving themselves, but you can show them how by modeling it. If your energy is depleted by doing things that are not yours to do, you'll have none of it left for your most important job—cultivating the self-love that will allow you in turn to be *loving*.

How do you cultivate self-love? This is a great question. In fact, one starting place is to begin each day by asking yourself, "How can I cultivate self-love?" One key to loving yourself is learning to trust that you have many answers inside you already. While you are learning to trust yourself more, here are a few additional suggestions to consider.

Get into therapy. If you want to address this pattern of codependency in your own life, start with therapy if you can. Engaging in therapy can help you to better understand the impact of your trauma history on your beliefs and life choices. If possible, explore with a trained professional how shame and past events have shaped your sense of worth. Telling our sacred stories in a safe environment is healing, and professionally trained helpers can offer key insights that we're not able to access alone. Educate yourself by reading about shame and the other issues related to codependency, such as boundaries, vulnerability, and self-compassion. I've included a few of my favorite resources in the back of this book.

Express yourself creatively. Creative expression is a powerful way of connecting with the most authentic part of yourself. Write, draw, design. Sing, bake, dance. If you aren't sure what creative activity you like to do yet, try different things. The reason creative expression is so important is that codependency is about the denial of the self, meaning that codependents are frequently out of touch with who they truly are at the core because their focus has been on the feelings of others. Creativity taps into a part of you that is uniquely *you* and can be a gateway to exploring what makes you unique. Also, when we're creating, we're less likely to engage in the default behaviors of codependents, such as worrying about how to fix our relationships or make others happy.

Set small boundaries and practice tolerating the natural anxiety that arises. To engage in any sort of recovery work requires that you create the space and time for that work. Carve out the time for yourself by saying no to an invitation or a request, and yes to therapy, a support group or inspirational event, prayer, mediation, daily journaling time, exercise, or creative endeavors. That exposed, uneasy feeling that comes when you set a boundary (and the pushback you can expect from others) isn't a sign that you're doing something *wrong,* only that you're doing something *new.* By actively setting boundaries in order to focus on addressing your codependent traits, you are doing the work already. The intention, the action, and the follow-through on achieving goals that are yours alone—these are the traits of a codependent person in solid recovery.

Develop a new relationship with your thoughts and feelings. Another powerful way to break the pattern of codependency is to learn to experience your feelings without judgment. This is not easy but is completely possible and is the most empowering work you can do. Pause for a moment and consider this: Your *feelings* can never harm you. However, your *thoughts* and *beliefs* about your feelings can absolutely harm you. This is amazingly good news, because our negative thoughts are all optional when we become aware of them, and our beliefs can be changed if we want to change them. The goal, if you choose to do this empowering work, is to allow your emotions to exist and then let them pass without ignoring or suppressing them. In order to achieve this, you must first change your *thoughts* and *beliefs* about those feelings.

For example, if you are feeling anger and your thought is that you shouldn't be angry, the harm is coming from the *thought*, which creates a sense of shame and a desire to suppress the natural feeling of anger. But if you notice that you are angry and allow yourself to feel angry (which is not a behavior, only a sensation in your body), then soon the anger will pass, as all feelings eventually do. This is a brief explanation of a complex and powerful way of engaging with your thoughts and feelings. I offer it here only for you to consider the possibility and explore it—not with the expectation that you will read this and suddenly be able to do it. Allow a self-compassionate part of you to step in and remind you this is a practice that will take time to learn. This is difficult for everyone. Tell yourself, "Today I will just remain open to the possibility that I can achieve this myself one day, too."

Be willing to keep trying. Self-love doesn't come to you in a single event or turn on with the flip of a switch. The only way to attain self-love is to commit to the practice over time. As you're learning, you'll absolutely experience moments that feel like failures. Perhaps shame shows up and rules again, or you find yourself in yet another painful relationship. It's a long journey for many of us. But if you keep at it, soon the tiny victories will begin to add up. One day, you'll look up and realize that you've arrived. You will hear the kind voice inside you more than the harsh one. You will see that being alone is not the same thing as being lonely. You will notice your ability to love others unconditionally because you have learned how to love yourself unconditionally. You will see words like *self-love, boundaries, authenticity,* and *vulnerability,* and your heart will burst with gratitude for what they've brought to your life. If that seems far away right now, that's OK. Just keep trying.

CHAPTER TWELVE

Thoughts on Losing One Hundred Pounds

My relationship with food, like every other aspect of my life, is a work in progress. Although I'd love to be able to tell you otherwise, there are still moments when I have to work to remember that the number on the scale or the label of my jeans does not reflect my success or value as a person. What's vastly different now is that I notice these moments, understand where they come from, and quickly forgive myself for the momentary lapse. It takes time to replace a lifetime's worth of devaluing cultural messages that target women and their body image. But I've come far, and I'll continue to intentionally replace those lies with loving new beliefs. I will never stop.

Four years ago, I lost one hundred pounds. There've been fluctuations since then, but I've kept it off. I haven't reached my goal weight yet, but I'll get there eventually. I'm in no hurry. My life isn't on hold. I'll continue to work toward that goal in order to honor my commitment to myself and because I know there's more for me to learn about myself on the way to that goal, not because I think being thinner is necessary for any other reason.

I don't have all the answers about losing weight, but I know without a doubt that weight loss is all about your relationship with yourself. That relationship is worth nurturing whether you're trying to lose weight or not. But if you are trying to lose a significant amount of weight and have been in the battle for a long time, just as I was, here are a few suggestions from my own journey.

Commit to a higher goal than shrinking your body size. Value your contribution to the world first, and then lose weight in service to that goal. Your contribution is how you decide to spend your time here on earth, where you put your energy, and who and what you choose to love. This could be caring for your family, serving God or whatever higher power you serve, or devoting yourself to a cause that needs your support—whatever lights you up or gives you a sense of purpose.

If nothing comes to mind, spend more time thinking this through before you try a new eating program. It's so important to separate your worth from your body size. Losing weight is a wonderful goal by itself, but women especially are taught to connect our worth to our appearance. We learn to not value ourselves and then wonder why no one else values us. We think we'll speak up in the meetings after we lose weight and feel more confident. We tell ourselves we'll get in the swimming pool with our kids next summer, when we're thinner. We believe we'll say yes to more social invitations once we're able to fit into our cuter clothes again.

The problem with this line of thinking, one I know well, is that after we lose the weight, we discover that we still don't speak up at the meetings or get in the pool or say yes to the invitations. The reason is that we haven't done the deeper work of changing how we will *feel about ourselves* during that meeting, or in the pool, or at the party. We become thinner versions of the same scared, self-silencing women and men. I did this so many times!

Losing weight is not the answer if you want to become bolder, more confident, more self-accepting, or more social. You probably won't believe me until you discover this truth for yourself. However, if you've lost a lot of weight and regained it, then you know it's true.

Or maybe you thought you regained the weight because you lack willpower or discipline? Nope. If you lost a significant amount of weight, you've proven that you have incredible willpower and discipline. If you gained the weight back, or if you simply became a skinnier version of your fearful self, the reason is that your body changed but *you* didn't. Until you do the work of changing your old, negative beliefs, you won't achieve the freedom that you think weight loss will deliver.

Consider renaming the problem. If you have tried to lose weight and haven't yet been successful, or you've lost weight but regained every pound and then some, find a new way of categorizing the experience. Instead of saying to yourself, *I just can't lose weight,* try saying instead, *I don't yet know how to process my emotions or change my negative beliefs about myself.* These two situations are very different problems that require very different solutions.

There's no shame in not yet knowing how to process your emotions or change your negative beliefs about yourself. Most of us struggle to some degree with knowing how to do this. Let yourself off the hook for not having skills you were most likely never taught—not because you weren't loved, but because your parents weren't taught, either. Start educating yourself in this area specifically. Work with a therapist or coach if you can. I highly recommend Kristin Neff's awesome TEDx Talk *The Space Between Self-Esteem and Self-Compassion* as another place to begin. Read everything by Brené Brown that you can get your hands on.

Increase your failure tolerance. *Perfectionism* is another word for rigid thinking, which is thinking there's a right way and wrong way to do things and that harsh judgment is the penalty for making mistakes. If you're trying to lose a significant amount of weight, rigid thinking is your number one enemy.

Perfectionism is about how we perceive failure. This perception dictates our actions (or inactions). Most of us tend to think of perfectionists as people who line up soup cans symmetrically in the kitchen cabinet. But perfectionism, when applied to our interior world, is simply a way of thinking that allows little room for self-compassion. Feeding ourselves requires constant decision-making, and there's no possible way to eat perfectly according to plan every day, so "failure" is inevitable and constant in weight loss.

Consider this fact: The only reason weight loss doesn't work permanently is because a person stops trying. Individual departures from an eating plan are never as catastrophic as they *feel*, but we perfectionists struggle to shake off the mistake and keep moving forward. Instead, we berate ourselves for not making the "right" choice. Our self-reproach is intense, and that becomes intolerable, therefore failure becomes intolerable. Instead of viewing a cookie binge as a forgivable experience and part of a process, we decide the lapse means we are lazy, are weak, or lack discipline. Or we may decide that the plan itself is the problem and abandon it in order to avoid these feelings. In truth, it's our *perfectionism*, not the cookies and not a flawed plan, that derails us. Practice making mistakes in every area of your life without turning on yourself.

Don't wait until you're thinner to start living fully. Your life, with all the wonderful and terrible feelings everyone experiences, is happening *right now*. Life isn't waiting to start when you weigh less. Don't waste another second delaying your dreams for a future day when you are an improved version of yourself. Challenge the lie that says you need to improve before you will be worthy of a full life. Accept the truth that you are 100 percent worthy and capable of experiencing love and contributing value to the world *right this minute*. Live as if you believe this is true and watch what happens.

CHAPTER THIRTEEN

Thoughts on Healthy Boundaries

Our relationship with personal boundaries—how we *express* our own boundaries to others, and how we *respect* the boundaries others set—is one of the clearest markers of our mental and emotional health. Learning to express who we are authentically, which naturally includes disagreeing with others and disappointing those we love, can be terrifying. It requires self-awareness, self-compassion, and emotional maturity. Setting healthy boundaries can trigger our deepest human fears—fears of rejection and abandonment. And setting boundaries can also threaten our most primal human needs—acceptance and belonging. These fears and needs, which are universal and valid, are so powerful that setting healthy boundaries can be one of the hardest things we do. So why learn to set healthy relational boundaries if it's so hard and stirs up so much fear? Well, you don't have to do it. Many people never do, and I say that with great compassion. But in addition to my commitment to myself to live authentically, I'll share the reason that motivates me. I've come to realize that if we *don't* have boundaries, we *do* have resentment. We may not be aware of it consciously, but others tend to know when it's there. Resentment has a way of leaking through, no matter how "nice" or kind we try to be outwardly. Resentment is related to judgment, which naturally leads to emotional distance from others. I believe that we each get to choose one or the other: boundaries or resentment. I choose boundaries because boundaries, as challenging as they are sometimes, allow us to love others unconditionally, while resentment interferes with our ability to access all that love.

The good news is that boundaries aren't something we're born with, but rather they're learned behaviors. Except in certain cases of unaddressed mental illness or extreme trauma, we can begin to learn the skill of setting healthier boundaries at any time. This practice strengthens our relationship with ourselves and creates satisfying, authentic relationships with others.

If you're new to the concept of healthy boundaries, here are some boundary basics—and a few reasons I'm a big fan of the benefits boundaries offer us.

What are relational boundaries?

Boundaries are decisions we make regarding what we say yes to and what we say no to, what we agree with and what we disagree with, in our relationships with others. Boundaries are also invisible lines in our minds that help to clarify what we *are* responsible for and what we *are not* responsible for in our relationships. For example, a boundary that can help us with our mental, emotional, and relational health—and one that most of us struggle with at times—is that we *are* responsible for our own thoughts, feelings, and actions, but we *are not* responsible for the thoughts, feelings, and actions of others.

Why do we need boundaries?

Boundaries help us protect our well-being, physically and emotionally. Living without healthy boundaries results in feelings of anxiety, confusion, anger, guilt, and powerlessness. My stories in the first half of this book offer some specific examples of this. You've probably experienced examples in your own life. Going through our days in this way is very painful and not how we were designed to live. Boundaries allow us to live with *less stress* by helping us to calm our inner turmoil, release unhelpful worries, and curtail our drive to control other's behaviors.

Boundaries help us to be *known*. When we draw lines and express opinions and also expect those lines and opinions to be respected, others see us as complete beings rather than seeing us only in the roles we fulfill for them. Women especially tend to struggle with this issue. One of the most frequent concerns I see with female clients, married or not, is loneliness. Many women give so much but feel completely unknown, unseen, and unheard. What's the source of this loneliness? It's not a lack of love from others or the need for a new or different relationship. The problem is a lack of boundaries. The better you become at setting boundaries, the greater the chances you will be fully seen and have your needs more fully met.

Boundaries help us experience and express *more love* for ourselves and others because they communicate respect for our most precious and irreplaceable resources—our time, our energy, and our mental and emotional health.

Why is it so hard to set boundaries?

Knowing where to draw loving lines in our closest relationships is extraordinarily complex. Friends with good intentions say, "Just set boundaries!" But if you're a natural giver, conflict avoidant, a people pleaser, or codependent like I was for many years, setting healthy boundaries can feel like you're doing something terribly wrong. And if you love someone with an addiction or mental illness, it's even more complicated.

Saying "Just set boundaries" makes it sound deceptively easy. Boundaries are the answer for sure, but they aren't "one-size-fits-all." Your general situation may be common, but you're unique, and so are the people you love. Your feelings and fears deserve careful consideration. In fact, it's important that you don't attempt to set boundaries with loved ones until you have developed self-compassion and have strategies in place for coping with the natural anxiety that will arise.

Boundaries are determined by roles.

The responsibility for setting boundaries in relationships is always determined by a person's role in the relationship. *Positional relationships* are those in which one person is in a position of power. In this dynamic, the person in power is solely responsible for upholding the appropriate boundaries in the relationship. Examples of this kind of relationship include doctor/patient, teacher/student, and parent/child relationships.

In a relationship between two people of equal position, however, the responsibility for determining boundaries is shared. These roles—friend, family member, intimate partner—vary in levels of intimacy, and, therefore, the kinds of boundaries that must be set vary, too. Relational boundaries in these kinds of relationships are more complex and challenging. Where the lines should be drawn and how they should be respected are mutually decided factors.

As a new friendship develops, for example, the two people—either overtly or passively—address such questions as *How often will we get together? Will we text, email, or talk by phone every day, once a week, once a month? What topics do we discuss? What type of humor do we both appreciate? What is to be kept private between us, and what will we share with others?*

In intimate partnerships, different issues must be settled, such as *How much time will we spend together, and how much time will we spend apart? When will we go out and where? When will we invite friends and family over? How will we come to a decision when we disagree? How will we incorporate our faith into our daily life? How often will we have sex?* Every aspect of a relationship must be negotiated, either implicitly or overtly. Boundaries—our personal choices and preferences that we express to others—offer a lens through which this negotiation can be viewed and discussed.

Boundaries are a learned skill.

Boundaries are first learned in families. For this reason, the ways boundaries were expressed in your family while you were growing up are the ways that will feel normal and comfortable to you. This is the trickiest aspect of boundaries: What feels most *comfortable* is not necessarily what is most *healthy*. In fact, the opposite is often true. As an example, I remember staying at a friend's house one night when I was a child and observing something that absolutely stunned me: In that family, even the adults left the bathroom door wide open when they were using the facilities. This bathroom behavior was normal to this family, but it wasn't the practice in my home, so it was uncomfortable for me.

As you consider your earliest assumptions about boundaries, you might start by reflecting on the unspoken or spoken rules for how doors were opened, closed, or locked in your childhood home. Doors are a physical boundary, of course, but they provide an example of how boundary norms differ from family to family. These familial norms represent our default comfort level with boundaries, a default level that will remain in place until we decide to examine it and choose differently. This is something that we may choose to do if we find that our "normal" boundaries may not be serving our best interests. Healthier boundaries are typically learned when we're in enough distress that we're willing to try something new.

Boundaries are based on our values.

Boundaries help to define who we are in the world. Making decisions about our beliefs and then expressing those beliefs requires a willingness to take full responsibility for our lives. Without healthy boundaries, we simply go along with others because we fear rejection or judgment. Defining ourselves in the face of this fear requires courage and the emotional maturity to understand what we value most and why.

Values are important beliefs that you hold—beliefs that shape your identity and inform every choice you make in life. The beauty of boundary setting is that it helps us learn who we are while we're in the process of setting boundaries. We become aware of what we're willing to stand up for even when there may be a cost to us. Examples of values include courage, generosity, pursuing personal dreams, keeping promises, treating others with kindness, respecting differences of opinion, protecting the vulnerable, faith, family, honesty, loyalty, commitment, and personal growth. The list is endless, and we each have our own unique set of values—some of which remain fairly constant throughout our lives and others that are regularly shifting and evolving.

Many boundary decisions involve an inner conflict of values. In such cases, two or more of your personal values are competing for the highest position. For example, you may value socializing with your friends and also value spending time at home with your family. You can't go to a party and stay home at the exact same time. You are sometimes forced to choose, and you do this one decision at a time.

How do you choose one important value over another? By acknowledging that each of your values is important to you but cannot be honored equally in this *one* decision. Choosing one over the other is not a global decision. If these values go head-to-head in a future situation, you may make a different choice. Right now, you're simply deciding which of your values feels most important in this situation, in *this* moment in your life.

As relationship boundaries go, it's difficult to imagine a weightier dilemma than considering whether to remain in a marriage or not. I've counseled hundreds of individuals who faced that question. And, of course, I faced it myself many years ago. When contemplating divorce, we're faced with seemingly unbearable choices between competing values.

In the case of abuse within a marriage, for example, the abused partner must choose between the value of *personal safety* and the value of *marital commitment*. Making such a choice can seem impossible and can take some people years to sort out. How does one choose between two values of critical and equal importance? How does one choose when both seem necessary to matters of survival and identity? The answer is, by clarifying one's values. Clarifying one's values does not make these decisions any easier. But the process does help the person struggling to identify the most pertinent questions needing to be answered.

Most people considering divorce, including me, don't do so from a place of abuse, but they too face a defining decision that requires a value choice. Which personal belief will they value *above all others?* In my case, I chose my mental and emotional well-being as my highest value. I've not regretted the choice, because I was clear about my reasons. I also respect those who make a different choice.

Whatever choice we make, we must accept all the resulting rewards and repercussions. One of the most challenging aspects of recognizing boundaries as an expression of our deepest values, especially regarding our intimate-partner choices, is facing people's inevitable judgment about our choices. Clarifying our values allows for some level of comfort even in the face of this painful judgment.

A decision to stay in or leave a marriage is only one example of a million potential life choices. What I love about boundaries is that they can offer us the gift of clarity about our personal reasons for *every* choice we make in life. When we're clear about our reasons, we can more easily accept the opinions and judgments of others without feeling confusion or shame.

When we make values-based decisions, we can act with conviction and also own the results. You can stay in the broken marriage and *own* your choice—taking pride in choosing financial security or the safety of your children or whichever value you decide to honor *above all*. Or you can leave the broken marriage and own *that* choice—taking pride in honoring your freedom or emotional wellness or what you believe is best for your children or whichever value you decide to honor *above all*. There are no right or wrong answers, only choices you make based on who you decide to be in this one life you were given.

Boundaries are about telling the truth.

A game-changing book for me was *Boundaries: When to Say Yes, When to Say No to Take Control of Your Life*, written by two Christian psychologists, Dr. Henry Cloud and Dr. John Townsend. After I became a therapist and was also placed in charge of developing emotional-wellness classes as an employee of my church, I became eager to understand boundaries in the context of the Christian religion. I had erroneously assumed that boundaries may not be encouraged within a religion where "selflessness" was a guiding principle. I was happily surprised to discover just how wrong I'd been. Dr. Cloud and Dr. Townsend base the principles in their book on the values of truthfulness and personal accountability and the right people have to exist as separate, whole individuals who have a responsibility to love each other.

As with all life skills that require emotional maturity, learning how to tell the truth about who we are begins with a strong motivation to do so. That's because it's not easy to do. As a personal example, when I made the commitment to change my codependent patterns, I decided to hold *authenticity* as my highest value, my guiding principle for making decisions. *Do I authentically want to say yes to this commitment? Do I genuinely want to spend time with this person? Do I agree or disagree with what's being said in my presence?*

Once I began to run every decision through this litmus test, the process forced me to become clearer about my own preferences, opinions, and needs. Then I had to learn how to *express* those preferences, opinions, and needs with kindness and respect, which is an ongoing art that I still practice today. Learning how to soothe myself when I feel exposed or judged after expressing an authentic preference, opinion, or need is also an ongoing process. When I perceive that I've disappointed someone because I have asserted myself, sometimes I still experience a sting, but it's manageable—and totally worth it. The practice has become much easier over time. In fact, I don't consciously think about these steps as I'm doing them anymore because they're simply a part of how I live now. The lifelong art of practicing healthy boundaries guides my life. While setting boundaries isn't always easy, it's not that complicated, either. And I trust this way of life completely because it's led to my ability to live authentically, which I believe is my highest responsibility to God and others.

The feelings of guilt and the fear of disappointing others are *real*. Until you learn to validate yourself when you tell the truth in love, you need someone you trust to cheer you on. The hardest part about living within healthy boundaries is accepting that we *are not* responsible for managing the feelings of others or their opinions of us. If we want to be known by those we care about, however, we *are* responsible for being honest.

Below are some facts about boundaries to keep in mind on the journey ahead. And on the following pages, I've included information on setting a values-based boundary with kindness and a four-step process for setting a boundary. When you're ready to start practicing, find a "boundary buddy," or contact a therapist or life coach to help you get started. I believe you'll find, as I and countless clients have found, that by setting healthy boundaries, you prove to yourself that you have your own back no matter what happens, and that changes everything.

WHAT BOUNDARIES ARE

- Boundaries are clear expressions of our own truth.
- Boundaries are planned actions driven by our personal values.
- Boundaries are markers of emotional maturity and responsibility.
- Boundaries are necessary for authentic connections.
- Boundaries are essential for us to know who we are and to be known by others.

WHAT BOUNDARIES ARE NOT

- Boundaries are not walls that isolate us from others.

- Boundaries are not threats yelled when we're at the end of our rope.
- Boundaries are not loud, angry demands for respect.
- Boundaries are not rigid, static lines of disconnection.
- Boundaries are not harsh, cold, or selfish.

SETTING VALUES-BASED BOUNDARIES

You have a right to draw the line after a boundary violation.

One common situation that you may find yourself in is the need to set a boundary after you have experienced a *boundary violation.* A line of some kind—physical, verbal, psychological, or emotional—has been crossed in a way you deem inappropriate or unacceptable. Because comfort levels vary with the person and situation, the process of setting boundaries requires that you know yourself. It also involves understanding that you have a right to draw these lines.

When setting a boundary in response to a boundary violation, having a trusted person help sort through your feelings and walk through the decision-making process with you is ideal when possible—and critical if the violation involves bodily harm or legal or ethical violations. In those cases, please seek professional guidance. In most cases, however, the violation is to our personal values, and this is the type of violation I'm referring to in this discussion.

Learning a process is different from seeking opinions.

Asking for *support* in a boundary-setting decision is different from asking for an *opinion* about what you should do. When you're offered an opinion, you only learn what another person might choose to do or say in a similar situation, based on their values. The more people you ask, the more potentially conflicting responses you'll receive. As a result, you may become more confused as you collect opinions from well-meaning people. You may later question the decisions you made based on what others thought you should do.

Once you've learned to use your own values as your compass, however, you'll know that your choices were guided by the most important beliefs that you held at the time of each decision. The four-step process that follows is designed to assist you in making decisions based on your values.

Gain confidence in your decisions.

In the pages that follow, you'll find a four-step boundary-setting process designed to help you when you're faced with this kind of values-driven dilemma. This process is *not* designed to help you make a "right" decision, because there's no right or wrong answer—only what you choose and your reasons for choosing it. This process *is* designed to help you make difficult decisions and live with the results.

The key to breaking out of the cycle of self-doubt and regret is to make peace with each decision you make, one by one. The peace you feel comes not because of a certainty that the decision was "right" or the outcome was smooth, but because you trust your decision-making process. You may be surprised by the confidence you gain as you allow your *values*, and not your temporary emotional states or the influence of others' opinions, to guide your decisions.

After you've come to a values-based conclusion about a particular dilemma, give yourself permission to be finished with the decision-making process. There's no correct answer, no path without challenges. If you remain stuck in the decision-making stage, you'll lose valuable energy, feed your self-doubt, and create more anxiety. You have the right to set this boundary for your own reasons, even if others have differing opinions about what you should do.

It may be tempting, if you question your decision or feel discomfort about following through with it, to go back and do the exercise again. Of course, you may do so if you wish. The danger, though, lies in getting stuck in a cycle of self-doubt and indecision. Allowing yourself to complete a decision-making process and move forward is a skill you can learn by practicing.

Communicate your boundaries with kindness.

Setting a boundary with kindness requires emotional preparation. A kind message is one that's delivered in a calm, clear, concise manner. Your kindness isn't measured by how the listener responds to your message, only by how you deliver it.

Setting a boundary with kindness requires you to carefully consider what you will say and how you will say it. It also requires taking the time to process your own intense emotions first. It's typical to experience anxiety while drawing a personal line with another person, especially if that person is very important to you.

Being kind involves acknowledging and attending to your own anxiety, anger, frustration, or other emotions rather than allowing them to drive your behavior. If you set a boundary in anger, the receiver will be more focused on your anger than your words. And if you set a boundary in an apologetic, passive tone of voice, the receiver may not take your message seriously because *you* don't seem to take your message seriously.

A boundary that's set in response to a boundary violation is an announcement, not an invitation for dialogue or a request for agreement. This announcement aspect of the process is one that some people find extremely uncomfortable, especially those who strongly prefer dialogue and agreement. Communicating a boundary is about sharing *your* experience from *your* perspective about what *you* need or expect or will do going forward. The receiver of the message has a right to their feelings, but it's not your job to manage those feelings.

One misstep that you will want to avoid is engaging in dialogue that devolves into an argument, thereby overshadowing your boundary-setting message and derailing your intention of delivering your message kindly. If you prefer not to engage in a discussion directly following your boundary-setting message, an approach I strongly encourage you to consider, you can prepare and practice a graceful exit line that communicates your willingness to engage in further conversation later.

After setting your boundary, you may feel anxious and vulnerable. It is *so* important to congratulate yourself for following through! Demonstrating to yourself that you have your own back in this moment is how you practice self-love. Even if the message delivery doesn't go as smooth as it did in your practice sessions, acknowledge your completion of a challenging mission. Setting clear boundaries, and doing so with kindness, indicates that you're living your life based on your most important values. Even if setting the boundary feels uncomfortable in the short term, you can look back on your actions and feel proud of yourself.

FOUR-STEP PROCESS FOR SETTING A BOUNDARY

Step 1: Clarify Your Dilemma

Describe the situation and boundary dilemma as succinctly as possible. The goal is to condense the entire history of a problem into one *current, specific* concern and a *single* question.

Example:

> **Situation:** *I'm a single mom and my twenty-year-old son is currently living with me. I'm*

paying for his room, board, and personal expenses, which I agreed to do temporarily when he lost his job three months ago. For the fourth weekday in a row, he has slept until noon, and I've seen no evidence of his attempts to find a new job.

Question: *Should I set a deadline for him to either find employment or move out, or should I not say anything to him about it and hope he gets a job on his own soon?*

Your turn:

Situation:

_____

_____

_____

_____

_____

Question:

_____

_____

_____

_____

_____

Step 2: Validate Your Emotions

This is the most important step! Skipping this step is likely to result in you communicating a threat or a demand—not the same thing as setting a boundary with kindness. Identify the emotions you're experiencing related to the situation. Emotions are typically one word, such as *sad, worried, angry, frustrated, disrespected, confused,* or *fearful.* Validate each emotion using the sentence format below. This self-compassion exercise will help you make a *values-based* decision rather than an *emotion-based* decision. Allow yourself the time and space to process your feelings so you can make your decision with more clarity.

Example:

It makes sense that I feel *frustrated* because *I don't understand my son's choices.*

It makes sense that I feel *guilty* because *I tell myself his lack of action is my fault.*

It makes sense that I feel *ashamed* because *my sister says I'm handling this wrong.*

It makes sense that I feel *terrified* because *my friend's son is thirty and still lives at home.*

It makes sense that I feel *lonely* because *I wish I had a partner to talk to about this.*

It makes sense that I feel *worried* because *my son seems unhappy and unmotivated.*

Your turn:

It makes sense that I feel _____
because _____
_____.

It makes sense that I feel _____
because _____
_____.

It makes sense that I feel _____
because _____
_____.

It makes sense that I feel _____
because _____
_____.

It makes sense that I feel _____

because _____

_____.

It makes sense that I feel _____

because _____

_____.

Step 3: Commit to Your Personal Values

First, identify the competing values, then choose and commit to the *most important* values on which you will base this *one* decision. Next, write down your decision and your values-based reasoning. And finally, determine the specific actions you will take to honor your other important values.

Example:

I value *my son's immediate comfort, my son's independence, and peace in the home.*

On the other hand, I also value *respect for my resources, personal responsibility, and natural rewards and consequences for behavior.*

My decision is *to tell my son that I will expect him to be employed within two months and* *begin contributing financially on August 1st or find another place to live.*

My most important value in this situation: *Natural rewards and consequences for our behavior are a reality of life that I honor. I believe my son must learn to honor this reality for his own well-being.*

How will I honor my other important values? *After I set my boundary, I'll commit to not complaining to him about his sleeping habits to honor my son's independence and my desire for peace in the home. I will recognize that my son's immediate comfort is a value I will always hold as his mother. I can honor myself for that loving wish while not allowing it to guide my decisions.*

Your turn:

I value: _____

_____

_____

_____.

On the other hand, I also value: _____

_____

_____

_____.

My decision is: _____

_____

_____

_____.

My *most* important value in this situation:

_____

_____

_____

_____.

How will I honor my other important values?

_____

_____

_____

_____.

Read your statements aloud. Allow yourself to feel confident in your solid reasoning. Experiencing mild anxiety—especially when breaking a people-pleasing pattern—is normal and doesn't indicate a "wrong" choice, only that you're human.

Step 4: Communicate Your Boundary

Write your clear, concise message in as few sentences as possible. Then add statements that convey empathy and/or love—if you feel those genuinely and they're appropriated to the situation—but not apology. Practice saying your message out loud. Your words may feel awkward, formal, and rehearsed. This is appropriate for an important announcement that's not meant to be a dialogue.

Choose your timing carefully. You might ask the other person, "Is this a good time for me to share something important?" If you don't have their attention, wait until you do. Then share your brief message in a calm, assertive manner.

Example:

> *When we spoke on February 28th, I agreed to cover your expenses temporarily. Today is June 15th. I'm glad to have you live here if you are employed. In order to continue the current arrangement, I will need you to contribute financially beginning August 1st.*
>
> *I know it's hard to be twenty years old and to find your way. If you need help in the job search or in managing this transition emotionally,*

please let me know and we'll work together to get you that help. I love you.

Your turn:

_____

_____

_____

_____

_____

_____

_____

_____

_____

_____

_____

_____

_____

_____

You may choose to close with a line such as, "Thank you for listening. We can discuss this more later if you'd like to, but that is all I'd like to say about this for right now."

Congratulations! You set a boundary! Now remember to treat yourself with kindness, too.

CHAPTER FOURTEEN

Thoughts on the Pursuit of Self-Love

"How do we love ourselves without becoming narcissistic or selfish?" I asked the first life coach I called. "I mean, what's the optimum state of being?"

In the early 2010s, after I was securely on the path to self-love, I began to seek out life coaches. I was curious about what came after therapy and recovery. How do we keep *strengthening* our mental health after we get past the trauma, addiction, and toxic shame and are functioning well? I had experienced having the *worst* possible relationship with myself; I wanted to know how to have the *best* possible relationship with myself.

Therapy had helped me integrate my past into my present, process my blocked emotions and traumas, and function productively. I loved receiving therapy, and then later being a therapist myself, for all these reasons. But therapy was only one tool in the mental health toolbox, and I wanted as many tools as possible.

The answer the life coach offered me on the phone that day?

Gratitude.

I thought it was an awesome answer back then, and I still do. Of course, gratitude was not a new concept to me, but I heard the idea differently that day. We hear the simplest truths only when we're ready to hear them and only from the sources that we've chosen. Gratitude gave me something to aim for as I moved further away from my old patterns. Although I wasn't aware I was doing it at the time, I was rewiring my own brain by consistently challenging and replacing my thoughts.

I used to think of gratitude as a still, quiet, contemplative state. I have since discovered, though, that it can also be a call to action. When you tap into gratitude and accept your own worth and place within the vast, timeless entirety of creation, you may experience a desire to give something back: not because you must earn your worth, but because you *know* your worth. Once you stop believing you need to achieve more, sacrifice more, or become more perfect in order to prove your worth, you'll see that you have a light inside you that's meant to be shared. Sharing this light is how we put our gratitude, and our self-love, into action.

Putting gratitude into action means protecting and nurturing your own light—God's compassionate love within you—and looking for places to share it. Those places are remarkably easy to find. But daily life puts demands on our limited time and energy, demands that will eat up every bit of our time if we're not able to say no when we need to, so we need personal boundaries in order to live out the commitment. This is the *opposite* of sacrificing until you feel drained, depleted, and resentful. Self-love requires you to aim higher by learning to nurture yourself first, then give from a place of fullness and abundance. As you nurture your relationship with yourself, you'll expand your own life and become a model for others to do the same.

If a little voice inside is whispering, *But isn't all this self-love stuff sort of, well . . . selfish?* then I suggest that you not ignore that voice. Instead, turn toward the question directly. Pause and ask yourself if *you* really believe self-love is selfish. Perhaps you were simply once told that loving yourself was selfish. That was then. Now you get to decide what *you* believe is true.

I'm quite familiar with that voice and that whisper. When I pause and address the question directly, I notice that the suggestion comes from the same voice inside me that whispers, *But wouldn't you be*

*more worthy of love and respect if you were, well . . .
just a little bit thinner?*

No. My answer is no. But only after I acknowledge the whisper, address the question directly, and
decide what I believe can I achieve clarity. No, I don't
believe that self-love is selfish. And no, I don't believe
that I'd be more worthy of love and respect if I were
thinner. But just because I consciously believe these
things doesn't mean the voices magically disappear.
Those voices get fainter each passing year, but cul-
turally encouraged beliefs take time and persistence
to change.

You get to decide what is true for you. What is true
for me is that I *do* believe that teaching ourselves to
honor, respect, and nurture ourselves at the deepest
level is our best answer to reducing the cultural epi-
demics of anxiety, depression, addiction, and suicide.
I *do* believe that the voices suggesting otherwise—
those self-worth-crushing beliefs that are so deeply
embedded in our thinking we accept them as truth
until we question them directly—are the more insidious threat to our collective emotional wellness.

As part of my own self-love commitment and
journey, I made a personal choice in 2018 to transi-
tion from providing therapy, which focuses primarily
on healing past traumas and the treatment of mental
health disorders, to coaching clients in the development and practice of healthy relational skills. Many

of my clients have traits and pasts similar to mine. For them, self-love requires ongoing, intentional effort, just as it does for me.

But, also like me, they're high-functioning adults who are not experiencing a mental health crisis and aren't in need of treatment for mental illness or intensive trauma therapy. They want to deepen their relationships with others as they strengthen their relationship with themselves. Some are in recovery from addiction or codependency. Some work in the helping professions—as therapists, coaches, or pastors—and strive to teach and model self-love. And some are parents of adult children who are "failing to launch," just as I did as a young adult. These baffled parents need support in maintaining clear, compassionate boundaries. All of these clients are among the most loving, extraordinary individuals I've ever known. They continue to need the reminder, as I still do sometimes, to turn some of that love back on themselves.

Personally and professionally, I'm grateful to, and in awe of, those who practice self-love so they can love others in the best way possible. Whenever I witness human beings aiming for the highest level of personal responsibility by caring for themselves with steadfast faithfulness, I'm overwhelmed by the abundance of love I see unfolding. I'm in awe of the divinity I see reflected in that beautiful, nurtured light.

This self-love journey isn't about crossing a finish line. It's about continually choosing to join this wondrous and terrifying human race. You join by showing up and fully engaging with your own life. You try your best to know and love yourself and others. You look to your left and right and see others on the path, all facing the same direction and moving forward at their own pace. You notice how each one pauses to help those who trip and fall.

Sometimes the person who falls is you, and that's OK. Next time you'll be the helper. And if you veer off the path completely, you don't have to remain on the sidelines. You simply focus on rejoining, and soon you'll see someone waving and smiling, welcoming you back. In case you've just joined us, allow me to be the first to welcome you. I'm so glad you're here.

NURTURED LIGHT

A former therapist, I now coach clients across the nation via video conferencing. Every day I work with intelligent, caring individuals who are committed to their own emotional wellness and to the health of their relationships. If you're a natural giver, a peace-keeper, a conflict avoider, a recovering addict or codependent—or all of the above like me—you too may need extra support and guidance as you learn how to identify and express your most authentic thoughts, feelings, and needs. Offering this support and guidance is my passion. As a boundaries coach, I specialize in helping clients cultivate self-love and set healthy boundaries so they can live authentically and love others unconditionally. We each have a light inside that needs to be nurtured so it can shine brightly. We can experience and share so much more love with this nurtured light.

If you're interested in learning more about the topics addressed in this book, or you'd like infor-mation about working with me directly, please visit www.nurturedlight.com. And if any part of this book touched you or prompted you to share your own stories, I'd love to hear from you at sherry@nurtured light.com.

RESOURCES

Boundaries: When to Say Yes, When to Say No to Take Control of Your Life by Dr. Henry Cloud and Dr. John Townsend

Conquering Shame and Codependency: Eight Steps to Freeing the True You by Darlene Lancer

Daring Greatly: How the Courage to Be Vulnerable Transforms the Way We Live, Love, Parent, and Lead by Brené Brown

Hunger by Roxane Gay

Untamed by Glennon Doyle

Mirror of Intimacy: Daily Reflections on Emotional and Erotic Intelligence by Alexandra Katehakis and Tom Bliss

This Naked Mind: Control Alcohol, Find Freedom, Discover Happiness, and Change Your Life by Annie Grace

Rational Recovery: The New Cure for Substance Addiction by Jack Trimpey

Running on Empty: Overcome Your Childhood Emotional Neglect by Jonice Webb, PhD, with Christine Musello, PsyD

Self-Compassion: The Proven Power of Being Kind to Yourself by Kristin Neff, PhD

The Untethered Soul: The Journey Beyond Yourself by Michael A. Singer

When Christians Get It Wrong by Adam Hamilton

This Messy Magnificent Life: A Field Guide by Geneen Roth

While I am not employed by or professionally affiliated with Rational Recovery in any way, I am grateful to have personally benefitted from its teachings. For more information about Rational Recovery and AVRT, the Addictive Voice Recognition Technique, visit www.rational.org. The book *Rational Recovery: The New Cure for Substance Addiction,* by Jack Trimpey, is available for purchase through major booksellers.

ACKNOWLEDGMENTS

My deepest gratitude . . .

To all the therapists, coaches, mentors, teachers, pastors, and friends who shared their light with me and helped me find my own.

To The United Methodist Church of the Resurrection for showing me that many devoted Christians are also fierce advocates for equal rights, social justice, and emotional wellness.

To my sisters for being my best friends since birth. It's impossible to count the ways my life is enriched by you both.

To my nieces for letting me adore you so relentlessly. I will never stop.

And to my awe-inspiring parents for always loving me anyway and for making everything that's good about my life possible. I can never repay the gift, but I promise to keep paying it forward.

ABOUT THE AUTHOR

Sherry Danner holds a master of science degree in marriage and family therapy from Friends University. She was a licensed therapist in the Kansas City area for ten years and currently provides virtual coaching services to clients across the nation from her home near Wichita, Kansas. She recently completed an MFA in creative writing from Antioch University Los Angeles.

CPSIA information can be obtained
at www.ICGtesting.com
Printed in the USA
LVHW111022100820
662812LV00002B/388